PSYCHOLOGICAL ISSUES

Vol. I., No. 2   1959   Monograph 2

STUDIES IN REMEMBERING

The Reproduction of Connected and Extended Verbal Material

by

I. H. PAUL

INTERNATIONAL UNIVERSITIES PRESS, INC.
227 West 13 Street   •   New York 11, N.Y.

Copyright 1959, by International Universities Press, Inc.

154.3
P32As

Editorial Statement

In the last twenty-five years psychoanalytic interest has ranged far beyond psychopathology and the therapeutic process. As Heinz Hartmann has put it, "We no longer doubt that psychoanalysis can claim to be a *general* psychology in the broadest sense of the word." The Editors of *Psychological Issues* believe that a new kind of journal is needed which will publish diversified source materials for a general psychoanalytic theory of behavior.

The Editors believe that relevant contributions can come from experimental studies as well as from clinical ones, from controlled developmental studies as well as from the genetic explorations of psychoanalytic therapy, and that investigations carried out without any concern for psychoanalysis may nevertheless contribute to the theory. In *Psychological Issues*, readers who are particularly concerned with psychoanalytic theory will therefore come into contact with important research not ordinarily presented in psychoanalytic journals.

Although the Editors have an important commitment to the advancement of psychoanalytic theory, they will try to make *Psychological Issues* interesting and relevant to investigators of all theoretical persuasions in psychology, psychiatry, and related fields. By selecting only monographs which confront fundamental psychological issues or that contain fresh and penetrating observations of phenomena, the Editors hope that the journal will be a meeting ground for all serious investigators of behavior.

The Board will consider only contributions submitted on invitation. There is at present no provision for consideration of unsolicited manuscripts.

Psychological Issues will publish four monographs per volume. These will appear at irregular intervals during the year. The journal will be sold mainly by subscription ($10.00 per volume). Single issues will be purchasable and will be priced individually.

Subscriptions should be sent directly to the publisher, International Universities Press, Inc., 227 West 13 Street, New York 11, N.Y. Editorial correspondence should be sent to the Editor, Dr. George S. Klein, Research Center for Mental Health, New York University, Washington Square, New York 3, N.Y.

CONTENTS

Editorial Statement   iii

1   SOME GENERAL CONSIDERATIONS REGARDING LEARNING AND REMEMBERING   1

2   EXPLICATION AND FAMILIARITY IN SERIAL REPRODUCTION OF STORIES: AN EXPLORATORY EXPERIMENT   9

3   RETENTION STYLE AND RETENTION ABILITY   61

4   CONCLUSIONS AND IMPLICATIONS   137

Bibliography   150

About the Author   153

Erratum   154

1

SOME GENERAL CONSIDERATIONS REGARDING LEARNING AND REMEMBERING

This monograph reports a series of experiments on how people learn and remember extended, connected, and meaningful verbal material—how they reproduce stories.[1] The major questions were: (1) What processes underlie a subject's reproduction of a story? (2) What properties of a story hinder or facilitate its recovery? (3) Are there systematic differences between subjects in the ways they retain and reproduce a story?

My study of these problems extended over four separate but interlocking experiments. The first was exploratory, the second and third were large-scale tests of the relevant variables, and the fourth was a replication and integration of the main relationships. Quasi-clinical methods (direct examination of memorial reproductions with free use of *ad hoc* hypotheses) were used in conjunction with experimental methods (control, manipulation, and measurement). Techniques for collecting, assessing, and quantifying such memory data were explored. In this monograph I will describe and discuss the methods, the experiments, and the relevant theories and concepts.

GENERALITIES, BACKGROUND, AND BARTLETT

Human learning and remembering is a vast but sparsely cultivated field of study. The rat's behavior in mazes and on jumping-

[1] The studies reported here were carried out while the writer was a Research Fellow at the Austen Riggs Center in Stockbridge, Massachusetts. He is indebted to David Rapaport for stimulation and guidance during each phase of the work. The preparation of this report was made possible in part by the grant from the Ford Foundation in support of research at the Austen Riggs Center.

stands has been extensively studied, while comparatively few experimentalists have investigated human learning, particularly the "everyday" kind, mainly because it eludes the usual laboratory methods. Methods that are subtle and supple enough for it are scarce, experimental control is difficult, and opportunities for meaningful measurement are rare. The clinical situation is still the best place for observation and the richest source of data and ideas on human learning and remembering.

The researcher who sets out to study memory faces two major problems: (1) What psychological theory will best guide his studies and lead him to worth-while observations and discoveries? A connectionist theory? A Gestalt theory? Or a functionalism rooted in clinical observation and practice? (2) What aspect of human learning and remembering should he tackle? Should he, like the majority of academic psychologists, study how people memorize lists of nonsense syllables or of unconnected meaningful material? Or should he study more complex phenomena like the assimilation and memory of emotional experiences? Is there a middle road that will combine the scientific rigor of the former with the meaningfulness of the latter?

TRACE VERSUS SCHEMA: WHAT KIND OF STRUCTURE FOR MEMORY?

Central to any theory of learning and remembering is a conception of the process which permits a person to act on the basis of his past experience. Ever since Plato compared memory to an impression upon a wax tablet, variations on the idea of a memory "trace" have been the popular way of picturing this process.[2] Descartes' variation pictured the "pores" of the brain being widened by the passage of "animal spirits" through them; according to Sherrington, the "resistance at the synapse was lessened"; and since Thorndike, connectionist conceptions of mental functioning have been based on this neurological model.[3]

---

[2] Gomulicki (1953) has presented a comprehensive review and discussion of trace theories.

[3] Connectionism refers to those psychological theories which assume that a process of elemental association is fundamental to cognitive functioning. According to this view, held by many learning theorists, learning is basically the establishment and strengthening of bonds or connections between elementary psychological

By the early 1930's, however, this model was being sharply attacked from several directions (e.g., Lashley, 1930), the most vigorous criticism coming from Gestalt theorists. The Gestalt modification of the trace theory (Koffka, 1935; Köhler, 1929; Wulf, 1922) postulated that experience is laid down in the brain by some sort of isomorphic process. The traces which result are subject to two influences: communication with other traces (*assimilation*), and stresses inherent in the trace itself, which are expressed by the Gestalt (configurational) principles, for example, *sharpening* and *leveling* in order to achieve maximum simplicity, symmetry, and good form.

In 1932 both the connectionist and the Gestalt trace theories were challenged when Bartlett, in *Remembering,* reported the results of twenty years of research on perceiving, learning, and remembering. He erected a broad theoretical framework grounded in a vigorous functionalism that is congenial to both clinician and experimentalist.

One of Bartlett's major theses was that cognitive functioning cannot be understood unless it is studied in the light of the subject's interests, attitudes, affects, and goals. He buttressed this thesis by naturalistic observations and by experimentation—data derived from models and methods which are closer to "real life" than the usual laboratory techniques of psychology. His was "a middle road." He argued that when psychologists use meaningless and unconnected materials as stimuli (e.g., nonsense syllables), and when they force their subjects to perceive and learn in artificial or unusual ways (e.g., by means of a memory drum), they seriously interfere with their chances of understanding everyday perceiving and remembering, and their conclusions will teach us very little about how

---

units (idea and idea, or stimulus and stimulus, or stimulus and response, etc.). Retention is fundamentally due to the persisting strength and reinforcement of such bonds, and forgetting results from their weakening or destruction by interference and/or disuse. For a detailed presentation and discussion of these theories, see Hilgard (1948) and McGeoch and Irion (1952). For a critical discussion, see Koffka (1935) who, along with other Gestalt psychologists, challenged the connectionist doctrine and insisted that whatever associations manifest themselves in learning are artifacts of the truly fundamental process, which is structure formation. Learning is not a matter of the establishment and strengthening of connections, but rather represents the repatterning and reorganization of cognitive structures—of traces. Recently, Hebb (1949) has shown how Gestalt phenomena can be handled by a connectionism that is based on modern neurophysiological conceptions.

people actually deal with complex, extended, and meaningful experiences.

With his naturalistic methods, Bartlett demonstrated what psychologists, particularly clinicians, have come to accept as a fundamental fact: the perception and recollection of complex, extended experiences are rarely literal or precise, but are regularly influenced and shaped by processes like "rationalization," "effort after meaning," and "fit," directed by attitudes, interests, and affects. He did not believe that a simple trace theory could survive the complication introduced by these influences. He also thought that there are fundamental difficulties in any conception that treats the mind as a storehouse of discreet traces.[4]

What Bartlett proposed in place of the concept of trace was the concept of *schema*, a term he borrowed from neurology.[5] Head (1920), together with Holmes, had defined schema as an internal postural mode—unified, and constantly modified by every incoming sensation evoked by postural changes—which furnishes a basis for the perception and recognition of postural changes. Bartlett recognized in this concept a valuable way to picture the operation of memory and of cognition in general. Bartlett conceived of schemas as internal organizations of past reactions and experiences which function as unified and active organs. A schema is an abstraction, simplification, and articulation of experience; part and parcel of its formation and operation are the affective aspects of the experience. An experience is not the resultant of incoming stimuli impinging upon a passive "clean slate," nor of the formation of isomorphic or literal facsimiles: rather it results from the interaction of stimuli and an already-structured, active organization of schemas. An essential feature of this conception is that the mind is conceived of as made up of schemas *about* the world rather than of images or traces *of* the world.

According to this conception, recall is not a reproduction *of* a schema, it is an active construction *based upon* a schema. While some "dominant detail" does persist, the major component of the original situation that persists is the attitude which was involved in

---

[4] For a discussion of this problem see Bartlett (1932, pp. 197-202), Koffka (1935, pp. 518-519), Lashley (1930, 1952), and Hebb (1949, pp. 12-13).

[5] Brain (1950) has presented a brief and lucid discussion of the origins and properties of the schema concept. See also Oldfield and Zangwill's review (1942/43), and Oldfield's (1954) attempt to show how *schema* can replace *trace*.

it. This attitude—broadly conceived—is the major determinant of the way the person reproduces the original situation. Bartlett showed how reproduction can be understood as an attempt to "justify" this attitude. The process of justification, variously called "rationalization," "effort after meaning," or "fit," points up what is active and functional in remembering, and what is integrative and constructive. It is certainly easy to find illustrations of this process in everyday remembering, and it is especially congruent with the characteristic mnemonic phenomena encountered clinically.

Bartlett's Work Evaluated

Bartlett's work had a surprisingly light impact on psychology. This is puzzling, because even today much of his book seems fresh and pertinent—for example, his emphasis on the role of motivation in cognitive functioning anticipates the so-called "new look" by many years—and his criticisms of other theoretical and experimental approaches are still cogent. Moreover, Bartlett provided methods as well as theory to encompass a wide range of mnemonic phenomena, particularly those pertaining to extended, connected, and meaningful experiences. To anyone interested in studying human learning and remembering, his work seems still one of the best places of departure.

My studies have been influenced by the shortcomings of Bartlett's work as well as by its obvious merits. The major shortcoming is that, aside from his broad functionalistic formulations, he did not speculate about process, nor did he conduct definitive experiments (those that yield a yes-no answer) concerning the operation of schemas. He failed to delineate precisely the nature of schemas, and never suggested how we might picture the detailed workings of the processes governing schema formation and operation.

This failure had at least two important consequences: (1) It prevented him from dealing adequately with the veridical and detailed recall that people are capable of—for example, memorization by rote. (2) It led him to overlook certain parameters of individual differences which, in the final analysis, must reflect the underlying processes of schema formation and operation. True, Bartlett recognized that people differ in interests and motives, in past experiences and expectations. But he did not concern himself with differences in ability to retain, and differences in the quality and character of remembering. Such differences can, I believe, teach us a great deal about the processes of schema formation and operation. To learn about these processes is the goal of the present research project.

A Summary of the Four Experiments

The four interlocking experiments reported in this monograph are part of a larger project designed to study schema processes in remembering. A brief preview of these experiments, touching on their main goals and findings, may give the reader a useful introduction to the project and the monograph.

The first experiment was a replication of the study from which Bartlett concluded that memorial reproductions are essentially active reconstructions based on schemas. Bartlett used the serial reproduction method (transmitting a story through a chain of subjects, like the spread of gossip or rumor), a technique that speeds the course of forgetting. The story he used for one of his main stimuli is an Indian folk tale called "The War of the Ghosts" (which I will refer to as the Ghost Story). In addition to being unfamiliar in content and style to his subjects, the story has many gaps and ambiguities.

My replication was shaped by two questions: (1) Are the gaps and ambiguities of the story responsible for the conspicuous distortions and fragmentations in recall that Bartlett found? (2) What role does the unfamiliarity of the story play in this striking collapse? To answer the first question I prepared an *explicated* version of the Ghost Story, in which I tried to ameliorate and reduce many of the gaps and ambiguities by means of text changes, emendations, and clarifications. Such explications should facilitate schema formation and hence promote the retention of the story. This explicated version, however, still retained the unfamiliar quality of the original. Therefore, to answer the second question I composed a story, the Secretary Story, which is comparable in many respects to the Ghost Story but contains more familiar actors and actions. These three stories were transmitted through serial reproduction chains. This exploratory experiment (presented in detail in Chapter 2) was designed not only to verify Bartlett's thesis, but also to look for clues to underlying schema processes in the reproductions of the various stories.

The findings showed that, while the three stories underwent noteworthy collapse and numerous distortions, the explicated version of the Ghost Story was recalled better than the original version, and the Secretary Story fared better than did either version of the Ghost Story. A close examination of the reproductions highlighted the integrating and articulating role that explications played, not only those which were experimentally designed, but also the many which subjects spontaneously introduced in the course of serial reproductions. Gaps and ambiguities seemed to be crucial places for forgetting and distortion, and were the foci of schema influences; this is where much reshuffling and rebalancing of material occurred, where skeletonizations (stripping, fragmenting, and segregating) and importations (the addition of material, often extraneous but seldom conceptually unrelated) occurred. From these observations I drew tentative conclusions regarding the functioning of schemas in recall.

The most provocative conclusion was that the importations and skeletonizations reflected two basic schema processes. The complementary neurological processes of *recruitment* and *fractionation* proposed by Hebb (1949) provided, I felt, a congenial theoretical model—a useful and appropriate way of conceptualizing the reorganization and articulation of schemas as revealed in the reproductions through the operation of importing and skeletonizing.

The subsequent experiments (presented in detail in Chapter 3) took their direction from the findings of the exploratory work and continued its quest. In addition to further study of schema processes, I pursued individual differences in manner (quality) of reproduction as well as in ability (accuracy and completeness).

Importations of new material into the reproductions—largely of familiar and explicatory material—which occurred so regularly in the Exploratory Experiment occurred with noteworthy frequency in some subjects' reproductions and much less frequently in others'. Some tended to import, others to skeletonize. I systematically investigated these tendencies and found them to be stable and general individual difference parameters. I came to view them as cognitive styles (in line with Klein's conceptualization [1951]) and interpreted them as reflecting some subjects' greater reliance upon the schema process of recruitment and others' upon fractionation.

I explored and tested methods for detecting and quantifying the presence and prevalence of these styles—particularly the importing style—and investigated their consequences for various aspects of learning and remembering by examining the serial reproductions of original, explicated, and familiar stories by serial chains made up of importers and of nonimporters. One of the main findings to emerge from these studies was that explication and importation were functionally related and often showed overlapping effects. I interpreted them both as recruitment serving to integrate and consolidate schemas. Skeletonization and fragmentation, which I interpreted as fractionation, could not be studied as intensively as importing. Still I was able to show that they frequently seemed to be serving an economic function, simplifying and articulating schemas.

These four experiments are presented in detail (in Chapters 2 and 3) in a narrative manner in which the discussion of background, conceptualization, methods, and findings are intermeshed. The reader who is interested primarily in theory and only in the broad outlines of the experiments may want to skip over those sections in slightly condensed type as well as the numerous footnotes. He will find detailed discussions of theories and concepts along with the general conclusion of this research project in the *Discussion and Conclusions* sections of Chapters 2 and 3, and Chapter 4.

2

EXPLICATION AND FAMILIARITY IN SERIAL REPRODUCTION OF STORIES:

AN EXPLORATORY EXPERIMENT

The story which Bartlett used so often in his memory experiments is a North American Indian folk tale called "The War of the Ghosts." Many of its episodes and themes are peculiar to Indian folklore, and to people not familiar with this folklore, the story is cryptic and the events seem unconnected. In repeated reproductions and especially in serial reproductions,[1] the story collapsed dramatically and underwent conspicuous condensation and transformation. For this reason Bartlett found it ideal for his purposes. He proposed that the distortions and elisions in the reproductions revealed the organizing influence of his subjects' schemas (their beliefs, expectations, attitudes, etc.): in so far as the subjects did not possess the appropriate schemas to deal efficiently with the story, in reproducing it they altered it in line with their available schemas.

Bartlett treated his findings in a quasi-clinical way—direct inspection of reproductions and *ad hoc* conclusions. He did not attempt objective or quantitative appraisals of the data beyond an occasional count of the number of words, nor did he attempt a further and more precise experimental analysis of the role and functioning of schemas.

[1] These methods are described and discussed below on pp. 15-17.

These two shortcomings—lack of objective methods of appraising the data, and absence of direct experimental manipulation of the relevant variables—determined the design of the present experiment. My initial plan was simply to replicate Bartlett's serial reproduction study with careful experimental controls, then to apply quantitative analyses to the results, and search for clues to the processes of remembering. However, the above considerations led me to incorporate into the experimental design two new variables —explication and familiarity—which are only implicit in the Bartlett studies.

Problem, Materials, Methods, Subjects

The Idea of Explication

Perhaps the best way to explore the hypothesis that the distortions, condensations, and losses in recall of the Ghost Story are caused by the disparity between the subjects' schemas and the story is systematically to vary the extent of this disparity and observe its effects upon recall.

One way to achieve this is to use subjects whose interests and knowledge are relevant to the story. An anthropologist familiar with Indian folklore would presumably be able to reproduce the story quite well, since he possesses appropriate schemas. We might use such experts as subjects and compare their performance with that of nonexperts. Or we might make people experts by teaching them about those aspects of a story that are strange and new—by forming the appropriate schemas in them.

Another way to decrease the disparity between schemas and story is to modify the story itself. One might systematically insert clarifying and explanatory words and passages into the text wherever it is cryptic and gappy, and thus build into it some conceptual or information bridges. This procedure facilitates schema formation in part by providing links to already existing schemas; therefore the clarifications and explanations themselves need be congruent with the subjects' knowledge and attitudes as well as their characteristic modes of explanation. For various reasons, but mainly because it is usually simplest in psychological experiments to vary the stimulus, I chose this last method.

"The War of the Ghosts" in its original form is as follows:[2]

The Ghost Story: Original Version

The War / of the Ghosts /

a) One night / two / young / men / from Egulac / went down / to the river / to hunt / seals, / *b*) and while they were there / it became foggy / and calm. / *c*) They stopped / their work / and hearkened. / *d*) Then they heard / war-cries, / and they thought: / "Maybe this is a war-party." / *e*) They escaped / to the shore, / and hid / behind a log. / *f*) Now canoes / came up, / and they heard / the noise / of paddles, / and saw / one canoe / coming up to them. / *g*) There were five / men / in the canoe, / and they said: /

"What do you think? / We wish / to take you along. / *h*) We are going / up the river / to make war / on the people." /

i) "I will not go along," / one / of the young men / said. / "I might be killed. / My relatives / do not know / where I have gone. / *j*) But you," / he said, / turning to the other, / "may go with them." /

k) So one / of the young men / went, / but the other / returned home. /

l) And the warriors / went on up / the river / to a town / on the other side / of Kalama. / *m*) The people / came down to the water, / and they began / to fight, / and many / were killed. / *n*) But presently / the young man / heard / one / of the warriors / say: / "Quick, let us go home: / that Indian / has been hit." / *p*) Now he thought: / "Oh, they are ghosts." / *q*) He did not feel sick, / but they said / he had been shot. /

s) So the canoes / went back / to Egulac, / and the young man / went ashore / to his house, / and made a fire. / *t*) He rested, / then he ate, / and he thought: / "I must tell / everybody / my adventure." / *u*) So he told / everybody / and said: / "Behold I accompanied / the ghosts, / and we went to fight. / Many / of our fel-

---

[2] The story is divided into its constituent themes and information units. The techniques for these analyses are described below on pp. 17-19. At this point I need only mention that a few objective rules of thumb were used to break the story down into its themes or episodes, and then the themes into smaller information units comparable to what others have called "idea units" (see Levitt, 1956, and also Clark, 1940). The themes are marked by letters [themes *o*) and *r*) are present only in the explicated version which is described below on pp. 33-36] and the information units are marked by crossbars: /.

lows / were killed, / and many / of those who attacked us / were killed. / *v*) They said / I was hit, / and I did not feel sick." /

w) He told it all, / and then he became quiet. / When the sun / rose / he fell down. / Something / black / came out / of his mouth. / His face / became contorted. / *x*) The people / jumped up / and cried./

y) He was dead. /

By systematically editing and emending this story, I prepared an *explicated version*,[3] the main expectation being that it would, on the whole, fare better and suffer less distortion and fragmentation than the *original version*. Examination of the two sets of reproductions might then point up some of the processes involved in recall.

The explicated version of the Ghost Story is presented below. The new and altered parts are italicized.

The Ghost Story: Explicated Version

The War / of the Ghosts /

a) One night / two / young / men / from Egulac / went down / to the river / *to fish* / and *b*) while they were there / it became foggy / and calm. / *c*) *They knew / this / was an omen / of ghosts.* / *d*) Then they heard / war-cries, / and they thought: / "Maybe this is a war-party." / *e*) They escaped / to the shore / and hid / behind a log / *f*) *But there was* / *no hiding* / *from these canoes.* / One canoe / came *straight* / up to them. / *g*) There were five / men / in the canoe, / and they said: /

h) "We are going / up the river / to make war / on the people. / *g*) We wish / to take you along. / What do you think?" /

i) "I will not go along," / one / of the young men / said. / "I might be killed. / My relatives / do not know / where I have gone. / *j*) But you," / he said, / turning to the other, / *"have no relatives,* / so you may go with them." /

k) So one / of the young men / went, / but the other / returned home. /

l) And the warriors / went on up / the river / to a town / on the other side / of Kalama. / *m*) The people / came down to the water, / and they began / to fight, / and many / were killed. / *n*)

---

[3] A detailed description and discussion of the explications is presented below in conjunction with a detailed examination of the reproductions. See pp. 33-36.

But presently / the young man / heard / one / of the warriors / say: / "Quick, let us go home: / that Indian / has been hit." / *o*) Now he thought: / "*My fellows / do not call / me 'Indian.'* / *p*) Oh, they *surely* are ghosts." / *q*) He did not feel sick, / but they said / he had been shot. / *r*) *Ghosts' company, / he remembered, / gives protection / from pain / and death / while the night lasts.* /

s) So the canoes / went back / to Egulac, / and the young man / went ashore / to his house, / and made a fire / to summon / everybody. / *u*) And he told them: / "Behold I accompanied / the ghosts, / and we went to fight. / Many / of our fellows / were killed, / and many / of those who attacked us / were killed. / *v*) They said / I was hit, / and I did not feel sick." /

w) He told it all, / and then he became quiet. / When the sun / rose / he fell down. / Something / black / came out / of his mouth. / His face / became contorted. / *x*) The people / jumped up / and cried. /

y) He was dead. /

The Idea of Familiarity—A Control Story with Familiar Content

The plan of the experiment was for each of two groups of subjects (Ss) to receive one version of the Ghost Story in order to contrast their performance and ascertain what influences the explications exert. Since the two groups of Ss are necessarily different, the experimental design requires a control story, one that is administered to both groups. Such a control story, aside from showing what differences (for example, in ability to learn and reproduce) exist between the two groups to begin with, can also be made useful in its own right by contributing a separate experiment variable. What variable can it most usefully study?

The explicated version of the Ghost Story, though more connected and somewhat less cryptic and ambiguous than the original, still seemed to retain an alien and unfamiliar ring, dealing, after all, with events and actions that are not part of our daily experience. Would this lingering quality of unfamiliarity still make it difficult for Ss to retain the story? (Is it still something they are schematically unequipped for?)

To answer this question (and at the same time to provide a control story) I wrote a story which, while equivalent to the Ghost Story in most of its formal properties (word number, information unit number, theme number, and roughly comparable in number of episodes and plot twists), nevertheless deals with familiar characters (its main actors are secretaries and the Ss of this experiment were also secretaries) and recounts an adventure in the present day. The expectation was that such a story would fare better in recall than either version of the Ghost Story. Its title is "The Sneak Attacks" and I refer to it as the Secretary Story.

The Secretary Story

The Sneak / Attacks /

a) Two / sisters, / who graduated / from business college / in Menasser, / decided to go / overseas / and work / in foreign / embassies. / *b*) They said / to mother: / "This way / we can work / and see the world / at the same time." / *c*) They separated / and took jobs / in neighboring / countries. *d*) "Promise / you'll write to me / every day," / they said / to each other. / They agreed / *e*) and parted. /

One sister / went to Montania / *f*) which she found / in a state / of war hysteria. / *g*) Her stenographic / competence / landed her / a position / as private / secretary / to the foreign / minister. /

h) "You / will have access / to top-secret / information," / he admonished her. / "I count on / loyalty." /

i) One day / she came across / a confidential / document. / *j*) It described / a sneak / attack / by the Montania / airforce / in which they were going to bomb / all / of the government / buildings / of a small / nearby / nation. / *k*) She read / the document / with interest / until she noted / the name / of the nation. / *l*) To her horror / she realized / that it was where / her sister / was working. / *m*) "Oh, I must write / and warn her," / she thought. / But of course / censorship / was invoked / between the two countries. / *n*) She thought / desperately / how to save / her poor sister. /

o) And then / she hit on a plan. / She would stop / writing altogether / *p*) and her sister / would wonder, / then become worried, / and probably soon / decide / to come and see her / to make sure / she wasn't ill / and need her help. /

q) On the day / she put her plan / into action, / she did not receive / her sister's daily / letter. / *r*) She wondered. / The next days / she also got no letter / and she became worried. / *s*) "It is very unusual / that she shouldn't write me," / she thought. / "Perhaps / my sister is ill." /

t) So she decided / straightway / to go and see / her sister. /

u) The distance / was only / twelve / kilometers / and she figured / it would be safest / to walk. / *v*) At the border / she met, / of all people, / her sister / *w*) who was coming to visit her, / she soon learned, / for the very same / reasons. /

x) That day, / both nations / bombed / each other / and the embassies / were destroyed. /

The Serial Reproduction Method

In serial reproduction, a stimulus story is successively reproduced by a number of persons, each one of whom, except for the lead-off member, learns not the original story but rather his predecessor's reproduction of it. This technique has a number of advantages over the method of repeated reproduction, in which one S recalls a story a number of times at intervals. In repeated reproductions, to secure substantial forgetting and transformation, a relatively long time must elapse between the exposure to the stimulus story and recall, and there is no way during this period to control the activities and experiences of S which may influence his memory: for example, some might review and rehearse deliberately, others unwittingly, others not at all. Since the serial reproduction method does not require a long interval between exposure and reproduction, in my experiments I kept the time short (fifteen minutes) and occupied the S with a concentration task to prevent review.

With only minor reservations we can assume that the serial reproduction is a valid method for studying individual remembering, on the basis of Bartlett's finding that the same types of change occur in it as in the decay of individual memory, but to a magnified and accelerated extent.[4] In individual retention the forgetting curve is usually a negatively decelerating one; it begins with a steep drop and then flattens out. The serial reproduction method capitalizes on this initial drop since it uses a series of first reproductions, the point where the greatest drop occurs.

The method has a number of pitfalls, however. Since different individuals necessarily form the chain, they obviously may contribute variously to the end product. This variance can be reduced by composing the chains of persons who have been pretested and matched

[4] See especially his discussion on pp. 171-176, and note the corroboration of Allport and Postman who found that "... the course of individual memory and of 'social memory' are in most respects parallel. The same pattern of distortion exists in both" (1947, p. 59).

with respect to relevant characteristics (for example, retention ability, style, and background). Another pitfall is that each S needs to make sense out of the stimulus (his predecessor's reproduction) and thus understanding and interpretation enter afresh at each step in the chain. This factor has never been experimentally controlled, and must be recognized as an inherent characteristic of the method. There is, however, reason to believe that such "understanding and interpretation" also play a role in every repeated reproduction (Katona's research [1940] as well as Bartlett's support such a position).

Learning and Recall Procedures

In all of the experiments to be described the stories were learned in the following way: S (always in the presence of one or more other Ss) silently read the story[4a] twice in succession. This procedure, adopted from Bartlett, permits each person to learn at his own rate. But it has the shortcoming that review and rehearsal are not controlled during the exposure of the text. To counteract this, the instructions emphasized that S should read no slower than his usual reading pace.

The learning instructions (preceded by informal remarks describing the research and emphasizing that no "testing" of the Ss either as individuals or as a group was intended) were:

> You each have a typewritten sheet before you face down. It contains a story. Please read the story through twice at your usual reading speed. Later on I'll ask you to reproduce it from memory to the best of your ability. As you already know, this is not a test. What I am studying is the story and how easily it can be remembered. It is quite impossible, I think, to remember it completely. But it is important that you do the best you can without straining yourselves. Try to relax and read it through twice in succession, carefully, but at your usual reading pace. Turn the sheet over again when you're through and look up. Okay? Any questions? Remember: read it carefully but at your usual speed and do this twice. *Please try your best.*

Reproductions were not made until approximately fifteen minutes, "filled" with a concentration task, had elapsed after the end of the

---

[4a] His stimulus copy did not, of course, show the information-unit markings or theme letters.

reading. For the Exploratory Experiment I devised a concentration task appropriate to the Ss, who were secretaries: they were required to proofread a manuscript into which various errors had been systematically inserted.

Recall was solicited by these instructions:

> Thanks. Would you now please write out the story you read at the beginning *as accurately as you can*. Try to write it at your usual writing speed. If you want to add anything at the end, go ahead and do so, for instance, if some details come back to you later. *Please try to do the very best you can.* Any questions?

THE EXPLORATORY EXPERIMENT

Ten female secretaries working at the Austen Riggs Center volunteered to be Ss. I divided them into two groups of five Ss. One group (labeled the O-group) serially reproduced the original version of the Ghost Story and the other (the E-group) reproduced the explicated version. Both groups also serially reproduced the Secretary Story.

Each S participated in two forty-five minute sessions during the same day, one in the morning and one in the afternoon. I tested Ss in pairs, one member of the O-group with one of the E-group. I administered one of the stories at each session and switched the order at each step (i.e., the first members of each chain had the Ghost Stories first, the Secretary Story second; on the following day the second pair began with the Secretary Story, and had the Ghost Stories second; and so on). The stimulus text was always presented to the Ss in typewritten form.

I knew each S personally and tried to create a relaxed, yet formal and businesslike atmosphere. I read all instructions, noted all comments, and recorded time intervals. The Ss sat at opposite ends of a large table. After the session I strongly urged them not to speak about the experiment to anyone.

Quantitative Analysis
METHODS OF ANALYZING AND SCORING THE REPRODUCTIONS

The usual way to divide a verbal text into scorable parts is to separate it into so-called "idea units." The size of each unit has, in the past, varied rather widely from study to study, and criteria have usually been quite arbitrary. Levitt (1956) studied the influence on experimental results of various breakdowns of connected verbal texts, and found that, while different breakdowns do affect the absolute value of Ss' mean recall scores, they have little effect on their relative scores or rankings. Nevertheless, it would seem desirable that choice of the units of analysis be based upon linguistic considerations and information theory wherever available and applicable.

In each of many exploratory analyses, I tried to formulate objective criteria based as far as possible on simple linguistic considerations. I made separate analyses of the word and group of words, of the sentence, of the paragraph, and of the story as a whole. I will not present here those that were cumbersome to apply and did not, in the long run, seem to contribute uniquely to the results. The following are the analyses, and the scoring, for the procedures that I finally adopted.[5]

1. *Word count:* All words, including "a" and "the," were counted.

2. *Information units:* The texts were divided into "idea" or Babcock units (Babcock, 1930) following the rule that each unit should furnish a piece of information which is not redundant, that is, not superfluous or repetitive in its context. Each reproduction was scored as follows: a word or series of words in the reproduction which corresponded to an information unit of the story, even if slightly altered (in tense or by substitution of synonyms), was scored *1*; a unit which was significantly altered yet preserved the sense of the original received a score of ½; errors, distortions, and units with no correspondence to the original received *no* score. The sum of these scores for each reproduction (*information score*) was taken to represent the amount of information accurately reproduced.

3. *Themes:* The stories were divided into themes with the guidance of the following two rules of thumb: (1) each theme should embrace a relatively independent part of the story—a separate episode, event, or major piece of information; and (2) a theme should be equivalent to an "ideal" sentence and no longer (that is, a theme should be stateable in one grammatically complete, simple English

---

[5] The redundancy analysis—a story-as-a-whole measure—is discussed and presented separately below on pp. 23-25.

sentence). Each reproduction was scored for the *presence* of the themes, regardless of the accuracy of detail or sense, by means of a list of questions.[6] Thus, for the first theme of the Ghost Story, I asked myself "Does the reproduction tell of some sort of hunting or fishing expedition or task upon which the men were engaged?" If "yes," then full credit for that theme was given even if *every single detail of the content was wrong*. The *theme score* is the total number of themes contained in a reproduction.

RESULTS OF THE ACCURACY MEASURES

The results of these three measures are presented in Table 1. The results support both of the major expectations:[7] (1) the explicated version of the Ghost Story fared better on all three measures than did the original version, being consistently more accurate and complete through the five links of the reproduction chains. (2) The Secretary Story, for the most part, was recalled better than the Ghost Story by both groups of Ss. In the case of the O-group it was unequivocally better recalled. However, in the E-group the findings are equivocal: for information score, and in all but one case (No. 1) for word count, the Secretary Story was superior, but the Ghost Story was superior (in all except reproduction No. 4) with respect to theme score.

Since the E-group recalled the Ghost Story better than the O-group, it must be asked whether this superiority is due in fact to the difference between the two versions (the stimuli), or whether this group of Ss was superior in retention ability to begin with. A comparison of performances on the Secretary Story can help answer this question.

In forming the two groups I attempted (on the basis of acquaintance with the Ss and with their secretarial ability) to equate them with respect to retention ability. Nevertheless, I felt that one of the groups did have an edge over the other, and so assigned to this group the more difficult original version of the Ghost Story so that an initial superiority in retention ability, if present, would be work-

---

[6] The complete list of themes for the Ghost Story is presented below on pp. 35-36.

[7] A comprehensive series of statistical tests that yielded positive results was carried out on these data after a replication of the experiment had been conducted with another and larger group of Ss (Experiment III). These results are presented below on pp. 106-111. At this point, however, no tests of statistical significance were made, but the data spoke clearly in favor of the efficacy of the variables.

Table 1

ACCURACY RESULTS OF THE ORIGINAL AND EXPLICATED VERSIONS
OF THE GHOST STORY AND THE SECRETARY STORY

	Original group			Explicated group		
	Word count	Information score	Theme score	Word count	Information score	Theme score
The Ghost Story	333	130	23	339	132	24
Reproduction No. 1	216	59.5	17	417	74.5	23
Reproduction No. 2	202	44	16	216	44.5	20
Reproduction No. 3	102	27.5	14	146	31	17
Reproduction No. 4	66	18.5	9	97	27	14
Reproduction No. 5	55	15.5	7	66	21.5	11
Mean of the Ghost chains	128.2	33.0	12.6	188.4	39.8	17.0
The Secretary Story	338	141	24	338	141	24
Reproduction No. 1	278	87	22	304	86	20
Reproduction No. 2	202	56.5	19	221	64.5	18
Reproduction No. 3	161	43.5	15	162	40.5	16
Reproduction No. 4	163	34.5	14	154	40	16
Reproduction No. 5	138	30	12	93	23	10
Mean of the Secretary chains	188.4	50.4	16.4	186.8	50.8	16.0

ing against the hypothesis. On the whole, the O-group did show a small superiority on the Secretary Story, doing slightly better on both word count and theme score, although on information score the E-group did better. However, compared with the large and consistent differences between the reproductions of the original and explicated versions of the Ghost Story, the small differences between the groups on the Secretary Story seem quite insignificant. We may still conclude that the explicated version was more accurately and completely reproduced than the original version because of the differences in the texts, not in the Ss.

The serial reproduction method permits only the lead-off members of each group to see the story proper, and Table 1 shows that the differences among their reproductions of the four chains are impressively in the expected direction. The question can therefore be raised: Were the effects of the explication and of familiarity confined to reproduction No. 1—i.e., are the differences between the groups due only to the effect on the lead-off members, or did the experimental variables continue to influence the reproductions throughout the chains?

To decide this question, I again scored each reproduction for accuracy, this time using as the standard of comparison not the original stimulus, but each reproduction's own stimulus story, the preceding reproduction. This analysis was done for themes and for information units. Table 2 presents the results.

If the effects of the experimental variables were confined to reproduction No. 1, we would expect to find no significant difference between the groups for reproductions No. 2 to No. 5 when each of them is compared with its stimulus story. However, Table 2 shows that reproductions No. 2 to No. 5 continue to show the expected differences. While the differences are not as consistent as are those in Table 1, the explicated version of the Ghost Story continues to be recalled more accurately and completely than the original version. A somewhat surprising finding appears in Table 2: the difference between the Secretary Story and the Ghost Story obtains only for the O-group; for the E-group the differences, though very slight, are in the opposite direction. This reversal, however, is wholly attributable to reproduction No. 5; in Nos. 1 to 4 the differences are in the expected direction.

Table 2

ACCURACY SCORES OF EACH REPRODUCTION, COMPUTED AS PERCENTAGES BASED ON EACH REPRODUCTION'S OWN STIMULUS STORY

	Ghost Story				Secretary Story			
	Original group		Explicated group		Original group		Explicated group	
	Theme score	Information score	Theme score	Information score	Theme score	Information score	Theme score	Information score
Reproduction No. 1	69	46	88	56	100	62	83	61
Reproduction No. 2	94	74	86	60	79	65	90	75
Reproduction No. 3	75	63	78	70	79	77	89	63
Reproduction No. 4	67	67	93	89	93	79	100	99
Reproduction No. 5	75	84	85	78	93	87	63	58
Mean of Reproduction No. 2 to No. 5 (omitting No. 1)	77.8	72.0	85.5	74.3	86.0	77.0	85.5	73.8

Analyzing the Text as a Whole

Any connected text has properties based not only on its parts (e.g., number of words, correct information units, themes), but also on the text as a whole. For example, a story has a structure which seems analogous to the form of a figure[8] (i.e., a story can be symmetrical, its "line" can be circular, linear, or multiply looped by digressions, and so forth). Since discontinuity can also be considered a property of the text as a whole, the structure of the Ghost Story must have been changed by explication. A thorough analysis should include an appraisal of the over-all structure and form of the texts and reproductions because such molar measures may reveal important parameters of retention. The analyses I have used so far, to show the relative accuracy and completeness of each reproduction, are molecular measures. A method had to be devised for scoring the texts and reproductions as wholes.

A story's redundancy—the degree to which its parts are repeated or duplicated in the test—is undoubtedly one of its important characteristics. Contemporary information theory emphasizes the role of redundancy in communication: it can easily be shown that a text with no redundant lexical elements is disconnected and meaningless. On the other hand, redundancy cannot be indefinitely increased without destroying movement and therefore continuity. Within these broad limits, however, texts can vary a great deal in redundancy, and this variation will reflect their over-all coherence and continuity. There is probably no one-to-one relationship between redundancy and coherence, because such factors as the complexity and familiarity of the text undoubtedly play a part—a simple familiar text requires and "tolerates" less redundancy than a complex unfamiliar text. This can be attributed partly to the presence of implicit or connotative redundancy: the fact that, for certain readers, certain words and ideas imply (are associated with) other words and ideas. This redundancy, which is so difficult to assess adequately, limits the validity of any objective method for measuring redundancy. However, with complexity and familiarity held relatively constant, it seems a plausible contention that, within wide limits, the greater the redundancy of a connected text, the greater its coherence and continuity.

---

[8] See Werner and Kaplan (1956). In her studies of retention Harrower (1933) also explored some of the figural properties of texts.

Since redundancy can quite easily be measured by objective quantitative procedures, it seemed to me to provide a foothold on which to begin an exploratory analysis of the structure of the stories and of the reproductions: to see what differences in redundancy can be detected between the original and explicated versions of the Ghost Story, and between the reproductions of the serial chains. If redundancy and coherence are indeed related, we may expect to find that the explicated version is more redundant than the original version, and that the serial reproductions grow progressively less redundant—especially in the original version chain. Since the Secretary Story is more familiar and hence less complex than the Ghost Story, it might be expected to be less redundant. The two stories differ in many respects, however, and we cannot draw valid conclusions about their relative coherence from their redundancy. We can, however, formulate expectations about changes in redundancy along the serial reproduction chains: namely, that the Secretary Story will show less of a redundancy decline as it goes through the reproduction chains than will either version of the Ghost Story.

MEASURING REDUNDANCY

No work has been reported on ways to analyze the redundancy of connected texts, so I improvised a technique for estimating the redundancy of word units. Redundancy is here synonymous with repetitiousness or frequency of occurrence, and word unit is akin to lexical unit.[9]

The first step in the redundancy analysis was the preparation of a distilled version of the text which omits all empty grammatical forms (e.g., weak conjunctions, articles, impersonal pronouns), changes the impersonal and passive constructions, where possible, to personal and active forms, and reduces the words to common lexical forms (e.g., "arrive" to "came-to," "returned" to "came-back-to"). In some instances this required the expansion of an ab-

---

[9] A lexical unit comprises a word and all of its dictionary equivalents, as well as its mood and tense variations (e.g., "amazement" and "surprise" may be the same lexical unit, so are "was amazed" and "will be surprised"). Furthermore, a predicate or verb with its prepositional form is a single lexical unit (e.g., "went-with," "smiled-at," "drove-toward," etc.), and abbreviated constructions are the same lexical unit as their expanded forms (e.g., "simultaneous" and "at the same time"; the latter therefore comprises a single lexical unit), and vice versa (e.g., "every day" equals "daily," "at that moment" equals "then," and so on).

breviation. For example, "warriors" was changed to "war-men"; since both "war" and "men" occur elsewhere in the test, such a transformation is necessary so that "warrior" does not stand as a unique lexical unit but is counted together with "war" and "men."

This redundancy analysis, then, is a special kind of *type-token*[10] analysis, since it reduces various types to common lexical meanings. It may be labeled a *lexical type-token* analysis. Moreover, it broadens the concept of a lexical unit beyond the grammatical and dictionary realm in that it links certain reflective and intransitive predicate forms ("become," "is," and the like) with their complements into single lexical units. For example, "became foggy" was considered the single lexical form "become-foggy," similarly "become-quiet," "is-dead," and so on, following the rule that such condensations are permissible when the complement itself can take a predicate form. Moreover, when active predicates seemed dependent upon their complement I condensed them—e.g., "made fire" into "make-fire," similarly "feel-pain."

In this analysis a number of words presented difficulties, and some *ad hoc* and perhaps arbitrary decisions had to be made. Pronouns, for example, offered a special problem. Since a pronoun usually represents a subject in an incomplete way, conveying only gender and number, it is difficult to know how much of the subject is being repeated (or made redundant). Moreover, the linguist speaks of a "zero pronoun" where one is not present but is implied by the grammatical structure. (Again the thorny problem of implicit redundancy.) Should these be counted? After some trial and error, I decided to count each pronoun as a full repetition of its referent and to ignore zero pronouns.

Once the distilled version was prepared, I counted each lexical unit and assigned a score to it, the numerator of which is 10 (arbitrarily chosen), the denominator the frequency of occurrence (e.g., since the lexical form "young" occurs five times in the text, each occurrence is scored 2). The sum of these scores for each text is its total *redundancy score*; dividing this score by the number of lexical units yields the average *redundancy score*. Finally, to derive an index that varies directly (rather than inversely) with redundancy, I subtracted the average redundancy score from 10 and called the result the *redundancy index*. I analyzed and scored each stimulus story and each reproduction in this way.

---

[10] The *type-token* ratio of a text is the number of different words in it (types) divided by the total number of words (tokens).

The redundancy index of the original version of the Ghost Story is 6.45, and of the explicated version, 6.73. Therefore, as expected, one of the results of the explication is increased redundancy. The Secretary Story has a smaller redundancy index than either version of the Ghost Story—6.11. This is not an unexpected finding, since a more familiar and less complex text probably needs less redundancy to maintain its coherence and continuity.

Redundancy Analysis of the Original Version of the Ghost Story

Underneath each lexical unit is its redundancy score: the number of times it occurs in the text divided into 10 (see pp. 28-29).

Redundancy Analysis of Serial Reproductions

Now we turn to a redundancy analysis of the reproductions to see whether there were any systematic differences along each serial chain as well as among the four groups. These results are presented in Table 3 (see p. 30).

A progressive decrease in redundancy index occurred in the serial reproductions of both versions of the Ghost Story. Only one of the ten serial reproductions failed to score lower than its precursor. No clear-cut progressive change occurred for the Secretary Story reproductions and their redundancy indexes varied within a narrow range; in the O-group there was a small steady drop in four of the five cases, while in the E-group there was a drop in three instances and a rise in two.

Of the two versions of the Ghost Story, the original version was consistently less redundant than the explicated version. Moreover, the differences between the reproductions of the two versions all exceeded the difference in the original texts. The difference between the redundancy indexes of the explicated and original versions of the Ghost Story itself was 0.28, while the average difference of the five reproductions was 1.06.

Before we can draw conclusions concerning structure from these findings, an extraneous relationship—the correlation between redundancy index and size—must be taken into account. Since the redundancy index is mathematically dependent upon the number of lexical units, the findings in Table 3 might be attributable simply to changes in the number of lexical units of the reproductions. The data, however, reveal no parallel relationship between the redundancy index and the number of lexical units; indeed a decrease in the number of lexical units frequently accompanied an increase in the redundancy index. This was conspicuous in the reproduction of the Secretary Story, where, even though the number of lexical units steadily decreased through the chains, yet the redundancy indexes did not. Therefore we can tentatively conclude that the difference in redundancy index between the Ghost Story and the Secretary Story reproductions represents a difference in their redundancy structure independent of their size, and, similarly, that the difference between the reproductions of the original and explicated versions of the Ghost Story also represents a real difference in structure.

What is the structural change reflected by the redundancy decrease? I have proposed that redundancy is related to coherence and continuity: for texts that are similar in complexity and familiarity, the greater the coherence of text, the higher will be its redundancy index. I checked this proposition by examining each reproduction, deriving an impression of its coherence and continuity, and comparing it with its redundancy index. This analysis (presented below on pp. 36-47) confirmed the close relationship between redundancy and coherence.

Thus the findings of the redundancy analysis fit nicely with the expectations, and complement the accuracy analyses in an important way, by showing that both versions of the Ghost Story, especially the original one, suffered a steady loss of coherence as they passed through the serial reproduction chains, while the Secretary Story did not. In other words, taking all of the quantitative analyses together, the Ghost Story reproductions lost steadily in accuracy and completeness as well as in coherence, while the Secretary Story lost in accuracy and completeness but maintained its coherence.

The accuracy analyses (Tables 1 and 2) were equivocal with respect to the differences between the reproductions of the explicated version of the Ghost Story and those of the Secretary Story—reproductions of the latter were not clearly superior to the former. However, the redundancy analysis reveals a clear-cut difference: the Ghost Story reproductions steadily lost coherence, while those of the Secretary Story did not.

Ghost's War

```
                        3.3  1.4
one-night two young men from-Egulac went-to river to-hunt seals
   5         5     2   .3       5       .6   2.5   10     10
then became-foggy calm (men)* stopped work hearkened
  5      10    10    .3    10       10    10
(men) heard war cries (men) thought maybe war men**
  .3   3.3  1.4  5    .3     3.3    10   1.4  .8
(men) went-to shore hid-behind log
  .3    .6     5     10        10
canoes came-up (men) heard paddles-noise saw one-canoe coming-up (to-men)
  2.5    .6    .3    3.3     10           10   2.5       .6        .3
five men in-canoe (men) said how-about-it (men) wish to-take-along (men)
 10  .8   2.5     .8   1.0     10         .8   10    .6    .3        .3
(men) going-up river to-war-on the-people
  .8    .6    .6  1.4       2.5
one-young man said (man) go-along-not
   2    .3  1.0   .3      .6
(man) might-be-killed (man's) relatives know-not where-gone (man)
  .3        2.5         .3       10       10     10           .3
(other man) may-go-with (men) (man) said turning-to other
 3.3   .3    .6      .8   .3  1.0     10      3.3
one-young man went other went-back home
   2    .3   .6   3.3    .6     3.3
(war men) went-up river town-Kalama's other-side
 1.4 .8    .6    2.5      10        10
the-people came-to river (the-people) began-to-war many killed
```

EXPLICATION AND FAMILIARITY

young man heard presently (war men) say let-us-go home quick
2   .3   3.3   5   1.4 .8 1.0   .6 3.3   10
that-Indian hit (man) thought (men) ghosts
10   3.3   .3   3.3   .8   3.3   3.3
(man) not-feel-sick (men) said (man) was-hit
.3   5   .8   1.0   .3   3.3
canoes went-back-to Egulac young man went-to shore house
2.5   .6   5   2   .3   .6   5   3.3
made-fire (man) rested (man) ate (man) thought (man) must-tell adventure
10   .3   10   .3 10   .3   3.3   .3   1.0   10
(man) told said (man) went-with ghosts (men) warred
.3   1.0 1.0   .3   .6   3.3   .8   1.4
many-enemy killed many fellows killed
3.3   2.5   3.3   10   2.5
(men) said (man) was-hit (man) not-feel-sick
.8   1.0 .3   3.3   .3   5
(men) told-all (man) became-quiet (man) fell /end-night/
.3   1.0   .3   10   .3   10   5
something-black came-out-of (man's) mouth
10   10   10   2.5   10
(man's) face became-contorted the-people jumped-up cried
.3   10   10   2.5   10   5
(man) was-dead
.3   10

* Pronouns are represented by their referents in parentheses.
**The "canoe men" were considered distinct from the "two young men," and therefore are not connected. The former "men" are italicized in the analysis.

Table 3
REDUNDANCY ANALYSIS OF THE STORIES AND EACH REPRODUCTION

	Original group			Explicated group		
	No. Lexical Units	Redundancy Score	Redundancy Index	No. Lexical Units	Redundancy Score	Redundancy Index
The Ghost Story	169	600	6.45	168	550	6.73
Reproduction No. 1	118	480	5.93	204	670	6.72
Reproduction No. 2	102	440	5.69	113	380	6.64
Reproduction No. 3	62	300	5.16	85	360	5.76
Reproduction No. 4	35	260	2.57	60	320	4.66
Reproduction No. 5	34	220	3.53	41	230	4.39
Mean of the Ghost Chains	70.2	340	4.58	100.6	392	5.64
The Secretary Story	162	630	6.11	162	630	6.11
Reproduction No. 1	140	610	5.64	160	740	5.37
Reproduction No. 2	98	430	5.61	114	530	5.35
Reproduction No. 3	85	380	5.53	85	380	5.53
Reproduction No. 4	81	400	5.06	82	350	5.73
Reproduction No. 5	75	370	5.07	52	260	5.01
Mean of the Secretary Chains	95.8	438	5.38	98.6	452	5.39

Discussion and Conclusions

The quantitative analyses show that connected and extended verbal material, of the kind used in the present study, tends to undergo progressive skeletonization as it passes from reproducer to reproducer along a serial reproduction chain, i.e., as it goes through successive stages in a hypothetical mnemonic series. Whereas Bartlett often used as many as twenty links in his chains (continuing them until the reproductions finally became fixed and "conventionalized"), the present experiment shows that five serial reproductions, obtained under certain conditions, are enough to yield substantial skeletonization.

One of the goals of the experiment was to devise and test procedures for objectively appraising connected and extended verbal material. The two measures finally used, information and theme analyses, were selected from a group of measures all of which reflected the progressive skeletonization along the chains as well as the differences between the experimental groups. They showed that the original version of the Ghost Story lost in accuracy and completeness, of information units as well as of themes, at a greater rate than did the explicated version; and that both versions lost at a faster rate than did the Secretary Story, though at some points the explicated version was retained slightly better than the Secretary Story. These results, together with those of the redundancy analysis, show a clear-cut pattern: both versions of the Ghost Story became skeletonized with regard to content and structure, the original version to a greater extent, while the Secretary Story underwent only skeletonization of content with no marked change in structure.

Thus a familiar[11] story, even though it loses a good deal of its content, maintains a coherent structure in reproduction, while an unfamiliar, strange, and sometimes cryptic story loses both content and coherence. Furthermore, explications, while they increase the coherence of a stimulus story to begin with, apparently cannot pre-

---

[11] It should be pointed out that, since the two stories differ in a variety of respects (despite efforts to equate them), it cannot be concluded with complete assurance that the property of "familiarity" is the efficacious variable here. Nevertheless, it seems safe to conclude, on the basis of this result as well as on the findings of other experiments—see, for example, the experiments of Tresselt and Spragg (1941) and Noble (1955)—that familiarity of character, setting, and event does facilitate retention.

vent its progressive loss in reproductions, though they do appreciably slow its course.

Explication and familiarity both refer to properties of the stimulus material that arouse appropriate schemas; these in turn, after some modification and organization, integrate a new schema which serves as the basis for recall. The extent to which subjects already have appropriate schemas, and the degree to which they are well or poorly articulated, will determine the organization of the new schema. If the material is familiar, as is the case for the Secretary Story, then the pre-existence of appropriate schemas is assured—the person is schematically equipped for the stimulus. If the material is strange, then schemas are not assured and the burden of organizing them is left largely to the stimulus material.

If the material is explicated, then schemas are, in a sense, furnished in the fabric of the stimulus. Perhaps the explications set in motion certain mobilizing schemas which assemble and organize the material whose schemas are primitive or poorly articulated. In turn, gaps or discontinuities in the structure of the material may interfere with the course of schema formation precisely because the missing information is necessary to facilitate the integration and organization of a new schema. When these links are missing, the corresponding steps in schema mobilization and organization do not occur, and we can expect little resistance to fragmentation. The present findings suggest that to the extent that a schema depends upon such mobilizing links, especially when they are weak or poorly articulated, it stands less chance of maintaining its integrity.

But it may be too early for this much speculation, and we will return to a consideration of these mobilizing or explicatory links and their role in schema formation after we have examined the reproductions themselves, an exercise that may throw further light on their functions. At this point we can conclude that schema formation and integrity depend upon at least two variables, explication and familiarity, and these variables may correspond, on the one hand, to those properties of the stimulus which facilitate mobilization and integration of new schemas, and, on the other hand, to the existence of already well-articulated appropriate schemas.

Qualitative Analysis

Direct Examination of the Reproductions

With the completion of the quantitative analyses our job of appraisal is not yet finished, for a careful look at the reproductions themselves must be taken. One of the questions such an examination may answer is whether the qualities and organization of the reproductions seem congruent with the various quantitative analyses, particularly the redundancy analysis—in other words, whether these measures have succeeded in capturing a tangible property of the texts.

A second goal of direct examination is to search for further hypotheses concerning modes and processes of schema functioning in reproduction. By tracing certain parts of the stories as they are transmitted through the chains (paying particular attention to those themes and information units which drop out somewhere along the chain, which come to be distorted, or which give rise to elaborations and importations), we may get hints concerning underlying schema processes and a better understanding of the role of gaps and explications in remembering. The serial reproduction method is peculiarly suited to this kind of investigation because it "freezes" the mnemonic process at a series of consecutive points. When a particular part of the story is omitted (forgotten) in, say, the fifth reproduction of a chain, it is often instructive to observe the changes which this part had undergone in the previous reproductions.

Since the direct examination will deal mainly with the Ghost Story reproductions, focusing on gaps, ambiguities, and explications, it is necessary first to discuss the original version and the manner in which I edited and emended it in the explicated version.

Explication of the Ghost Story

My first problem in editing the Ghost Story was to locate its important gaps. Having no objective way to define a "gap," I had to rely on subjective and "common sense" judgment. I located two major gaps in the texts: (1) In theme p) the young man suddenly and inexplicably comes to the dramatic conclusion that his companions "are ghosts"; (2) theme q) contains the enigmatic phrase "he did not feel sick, but . . . he had been shot."

To "fill" these gaps, I wrote two new themes: (1) The fact that he is called "Indian" is made to explain how it is that the young man realizes that the warriors are not like his fellows (incorporated into theme *o*) in the explicated version); (2) the fact that he is with ghosts is made to explain his insensitivity to pain and protection from death [this became theme *r*) of the explicated version]. This second explication, by saying that the protection is supposed to last only through that night, also prepares for the climax of the story: the death of the young man at sunrise.

In the version of the story which Bartlett used, theme *c*) is not present: the mention of "foggy and calm" is followed immediately by the war-cries, and the young men react by fleeing and hiding. There seems to be an implicit gap here because it somehow *feels* as if the "foggy and calm" is an omen of some sort. Therefore an explication seemed in order following theme *b*), to spell out the omen implied by the "foggy and calm" and therefore account for the men's flight. This explication could also help to prepare for the man's later realization that the warriors are ghosts. Theme *c*) in the explicated version was designed to fulfill these two purposes. In order to make the text of the original version equivalent, a new theme needed to be added there, and so for the original version I wrote another theme *c*) which added verbal material but not explication.

These were the three major alterations of the story. In addition, I made the following smaller changes and additions:

1. In theme *a*): "*to hunt seals* in the river" seemed unfamiliar, so I substituted "*to fish.*"

2. Theme *f*) gave another opportunity to emphasize the supernatural nature of the war party. Why is it that the hiding is to no avail? Because from "*these*" canoes there is no way to conceal oneself.

3. Themes *g*) and *h*) seem to join better when *h*) precedes *g*), and were therefore reversed in the explicated version.

4. In theme *j*): why the other man can go is unexplained in the original. A possible reason, suggested in part by the excuse which the first man makes, is that he has no relatives.

5. In theme *p*): the word "surely" is inserted for added stress.

6. Since theme *r*) adds fourteen words and six information units to the explicated version, it was necessary to add some text to the original version in order to make it equivalent. Therefore theme *t*), which also contains fourteen words and six information units but does not seem to explicate the story, was added to the original version.

EXPLICATION AND FAMILIARITY

Finally, in order to reduce the two versions to the dimensions of the story as Bartlett used it (to make the study an approximate replication of his), I omitted a part of the original story in which the young men protest that they have no arrows and the warriors answer that there are arrows in the canoes.

Theme Analysis of the Ghost Story

Since the unit of observation was the theme, here are the titles and the scoring criteria of the themes of the two versions of the Ghost Story. Those which are unique to the original version are marked with asterisks (*), and those unique to the explicated versions with daggers (†).

THEME ANALYSIS OF GHOST STORY

Theme a)	THE HUNT:	Does the reproduction tell of a hunting or fishing expedition by the men?
Theme b)	ATMOSPHERE:	Is some mention made of the atmospheric conditions?
Theme c)	CEASE WORK:	Is it mentioned that they stop and/or listen?*
†Theme c)	SOMETHING UP:	Is there some portent given of something pending?†
Theme d)	SOMETHING HEARD:	Does the reproduction mention that they heard something approaching (war-cries or sounds of canoes)?
Theme e)	HIDING:	Do the men hide in some way?
Theme f)	ACCOSTED:	Is there some description of the canoes approaching the men?
Theme g)	INVITATION:	Is there mention of an invitation?
Theme h)	WAR-PLANS:	Are the plans of the men in the boat mentioned?
Theme i)	REFUSAL:	Is one man's refusal mentioned?
Theme j)	PERMISSION:	Does he in some way allow or encourage the other to go?
Theme k)	SEPARATION:	Is it mentioned that one goes and not the other?

Theme l)	WAR-TRIP:	Is the traveling in the canoes mentioned?
Theme m)	FIGHT:	Is the battle mentioned or described?
Theme n)	"RETREAT":	Is it described that someone cries for the battle to cease (it is sufficient that someone cries out to bring attention to the casualty)?
†*Theme o)*	"INDIAN":	Is it mentioned that he is never called "Indian" by his people or that there is something noteworthy about it?†
Theme p)	REALIZATION:	Is it mentioned that the man realizes he is in the company of ghosts?
Theme q)	ENIGMA:	Is it mentioned that he is wounded yet feels no pain?
†*Theme r)*	PROTECTION:	Is his knowledge of ghosts' protection mentioned?†
Theme s)	HOME:	Is the return home or to his people mentioned?
**Theme t)*	DECISION TO TELL:	Is there some mention of his decision to tell his adventure?*
Theme u)	REVELATIONS:	Is it described how he tells everyone about his adventure?
Theme v)	ENIGMA AGAIN:	Is the enigma recounted?
Theme w)	SOMETHING BLACK:	Is there a description of the morning events (any one of the strange afflictions will do)?
Theme x)	REACTION:	Is the reaction of sorrow and/or horror by the people mentioned?
Theme y)	DEATH:	Is the man's death mentioned?

Quality and Structure of the Reproductions

My first examination was to gain an impression of qualitative and structural aspects of each reproduction as a whole, beginning with the reproductions of the two versions of the Ghost Story which are presented below. Themes are lettered according to the theme

EXPLICATION AND FAMILIARITY

analysis of the stimulus story, and noteworthy changes, distortions, and importations are italicized.

SERIAL REPRODUCTIONS OF THE ORIGINAL VERSION OF THE GHOST STORY

REPRODUCTION NO. 1

The War of the Ghosts

a) One night two young men from Ebaga went hunting for seals. *b*) While they were there the night became foggy and calm. *d*) They heard the sound of muffled oars. They said, "Perhaps this is a war party." *e*) They went ashore and hid behind a log. *f*) Soon a boat appeared. *h*) The men in it said, "We are going to make war on the people up the river." *The two men discussed who should go, k*) finally one went with them and the other went home.

When they reached the place, *m*) many men came down to the shore. Many on each side were killed. *n*) Finally, someone said, "That Indian is shot." *q*) The man did not feel anything, though told he was hit.

s) When the young man reached home he went ashore and lit a fire. *t*) He said to himself, "I must tell everyone about my adventures." *u*) He called his friends and told them about the battle, saying that many men on both sides had been killed *p*) and that *he had discovered that the men he was fighting on the same side as, were ghosts. v*) He told them he had been shot but not hurt.

w) When the morning came the young man grew pale. Something black came out of his mouth. *y*) He fell down. He was dead.

REPRODUCTION NO. 2

a) Two men *were fishing. d*) Suddenly they heard the sound of oars *b*) *through the fog.* One said, "Maybe it is a war party." *e*) They hid behind a log *f*) and saw the men in the boat. *h*) One man said, "We are going to attack another village up the river." *k*) One man decided to go and the other went home.

The first man traveled with the men in the boat *m*) and when they landed a lot of men came down to the river's edge and there was a terrific battle. A lot of men were killed on both sides. *n*) Suddenly one man said, "The Indian has been shot." *q*) The man didn't feel any pain.

s) He went home, built a large fire, *u*) and called all his friends to tell them of his experiences. He said there was a big battle, a lot of men were killed, *v*) and the men said he was shot. He didn't believe it because he couldn't feel anything. *p*) *He said, "They must have been ghosts!"*

w) The next morning he woke up and was sick. Black stuff fell out of his mouth, *y*) He fell down. He was dead.

(The men were from the village of Aboga.)

REPRODUCTION NO. 3

a) Two men were fishing. *d*) They heard a boat come up the river *b*) in the fog and saw men in it. *e*) They hid behind a log. *h*) The men in the boat were going to attack a village up the stream. *k*) One of the fishermen joined them.

m) They attacked a village and several people were killed. *n*) Suddenly one said, "The Indian is shot."

s) He returned home *u*) and told his friends about his experience. *v*) They told him he was shot but he didn't believe them.

w) In the morning he was sick and spit up black stuff. *y*) He died. *p*)"They must have been ghosts," he said.

REPRODUCTION NO. 4

a) Two men were fishing. *f*) A boat full of men came up the river. *e*) The men hid behind a log. *m*) The men in the boat attacked a village upstream. *k*) One of the men joined them.

In the attack some people were killed. *n*) Someone said: "The Indian is shot."

w) He was sick the next morning and spit up some black stuff *y*) and died.

p) *"They must have been ghosts."*

REPRODUCTION NO. 5

a) Two men were fishing. *f*) They saw a canoe approaching. *e*) The two men hid behind a log.

m) The men went up river and attacked a town. *k*) One of the fishermen joined them.

Someone said, *"They must be Indians."*

w) The next day the man grew ill and bled some black stuff.

p) *"He must have been a ghost."*

SERIAL REPRODUCTIONS OF THE EXPLICATED VERSION OF THE GHOST STORY

REPRODUCTION NO. 1

The War of the Ghosts

a) One night two men of Egulac went to the river to go fishing. *b*) While they were there the night became foggy and calm *c*) and they knew that this denoted that ghosts were nearby, *as this was the sort of night on which they would appear.*

d) Suddenly from out of the fog they perceived canoes approaching and in terror *e*) hid behind a log on the shore. *f*) They soon realized that there was no hiding, for one of the canoes came steadily toward them. *g*) From the canoe stepped a man who said, "You two *must* come with us, *h*) as we are about to make war on *your neighbors.*" The two fishermen then noted that the canoe held five men. *i*) On hearing this remark from the man in the canoe, one of the fishermen cried out, "Oh, no, I cannot go with you, I have a family and relatives *whom I must care for.*" *j*) He then turned to his companion and said, "But you can go, you have *no one dependent on you.*" *k*) So the second of the two fishermen entered the canoe with the five men.

l) After some traveling they reached the land of Kalama, which they had been told was their destination. *m)* A great battle ensued, many people on both sides being killed. *n)* Suddenly the fisherman heard one of his companions shout, "We must leave at once! The Indian has been hit!" *o)* This was heard with considerable surprise by the fisherman as *he knew he was not an Indian. q)* Also *he was amazed* that he had felt no pain, though he knew he had been hit and that his companions meant him when they mentioned "Indian." Then he realized that he felt no pain because *p)* he was with ghosts *and not men, r)* that explained his inability to feel pain. Also that this *magic* was good only for the night and that in the morning he would die.

s) Whereupon his companions took him back to his people and he made a great fire that called them all together. *u)* He rose amidst them and told them the story of the battle. "I was taken to a neighboring land where a great battle took place. *v)* I was called Indian and was wounded, but felt it not. Many, many people were killed on both sides."

At that moment the sun rose. The man who had told the story stood. *w)* He began to shake and fell upon the ground. Something black poured from his mouth.

y) He was dead.

REPRODUCTION NO. 2

Two men *were on the beach. b)* The night was foggy and calm—*c)* a night on which ghosts were likely to appear. *d)* Suddenly the two men heard something approach *e)* and they ran up onto the beach and *tried* to hide behind a log. *f)* They soon found there was no hiding as the canoes continued to approach. *g)* A man stepped out of the canoe and asked the two men to accompany him. *i)* The first fisherman replied that he could not go as he had a wife and relatives for whom he was obliged to care. *j)* He urged the second fisherman to go as he had no one dependent upon him. *k)* The second fisherman went. *l)* They journeyed to Kalama. *m)* War ensued. *n)* The fisherman heard one of the men say. "The Indian has been hit." *o)* He could not understand this as he was not an Indian and yet he knew they referred to him as he had been hit. *g)* Further, *he was puzzled* because he felt no pain from his wound. *p)* Then he recalled he was among ghosts and, *r)* therefore, felt no pain. He realized, however, that when morning came, the ghosts would leave and he would die. *s)* He returned to his people *u)* and told them his story. *w)* He fell over, something black poured from his mouth—*y)* he was dead.

REPRODUCTION NO. 3

Two men were sitting on a beach. *d)* They heard a noise *but couldn't see anything b)* because of the fog. *f)* The canoe came up to shore and a man got out. *g)* He asked the two fishermen to come to Tralama with him. *i)* The first fisherman refused because he had a wife and relatives to support. *k)* The second fisherman was independent and he went with him. *l)* They went away in the boat to Tralama. *m)* War ensued. *n)* He could hear somebody say, "The Indian has been hit." *o)* He couldn't see any Indian and he knew they must be talking about him. *q*) He didn't feel any pain *p*) but then remembered that he was *in a land of ghosts r*) so that he wouldn't feel anything. *s*) He came back to his friends *u*) and told them the story. *w*) All of a sudden something black came out of his mouth *y*) and he fell over—dead.

REPRODUCTION NO. 4

a) Two fishermen *were fishing off shore. f*) A boat came to shore and a man got out. *g*) He asked them to come with him to Tralama. *i*) The first fisherman refused, since he had a wife and children *waiting for him. k*) The second fisherman was independent and so went with him *l*) to Tralama. *m*) War ensued. *n*) He heard someone say "The Indian has been hit." *q*) He felt no pain *p*) but knew he was in a land of ghosts. *s*) He returned to his friends *u*) to tell them the story. *w*) Something black came out of his mouth *y*) and he dropped over—dead.

REPRODUCTION NO. 5

a) Two fishermen were fishing off shore. *f*) A man came up *g*) and asked them to go out with him. *i*) One refused because he had a wife and children. *k*) The other went with him because he had no one. *l*) They went to Tralama. *m*) War ensued. *n*) Someone cried, "The Indian *is dead*." He was hit and *p*) *there were ghosts. w*) Something black fell out of his mouth *y*) and he was dead.

To begin with reproductions No. 5, and proceed backward along the chains (later we will retrace our steps to follow particular themes and information units as they are transmitted along the chains): The first impression about the two final reproductions is that the reproduction of the explicated version is more coherent and continuous. This impression is reflected in the redundancy indexes of these two reproductions as shown in Table 3: the explicated version reproduction is substantially more redundant than the original version reproduction (4.39 to 3.53). The explicated version reproduction, though only eleven words longer, is comparatively tight and retains the core of the Ghost Story, while the original version reproduction is fragmentary and has lost the core of the story. It is easy to detect three large gaps in this reproduction: theme *m*) is entirely disconnected; and the sentence, "Someone said, 'they must be Indians,' " is isolated both from what precedes and what follows it. On the other hand, No. 5 of the explicated version contains only a minor gap at theme *p*), which, although joined in a sentence with "he was hit," seems to stand apart.

The difference in structure between reproductions of the original and explicated versions is especially conspicuous in reproductions

No. 4. The largest difference in redundancy index between any pair of reproductions exists between these two: 2.57 to 4.66. Explicated version reproduction No. 4 is quite coherent and flowing, and tells the story well in spite of the reduction in content. Theme p), though not quite as isolated as in No. 5, is nonetheless poorly integrated. Original version reproduction No. 4, on the other hand, is disjointed: there are major breaks in the story line, particularly between themes o) and m) and between themes n) and w), and theme p) is merely tacked on at the end.

The beginnings of the fragmented character of the original version reproductions become apparent in No. 3, a choppy and staccato account which contains a number of ambiguities. For example, theme v): who "told him he was shot," his "friends" or the warriors? And why was it that "he didn't believe them"? Theme p), which is merely appended to the text, is unconnected and ambiguous—who "must have been ghosts"? And how could "he" say this when "he died" in the previous sentence? Gaps are also present between themes e) and h) and s). On the other hand, explicated version reproduction No. 3 is coherent, rather tightly constructed, and relatively free of ambiguity. Its redundancy index, however, does not seem fully to reflect this difference (it is 5.76 compared to original version reproduction No. 3 of 5.16, the smallest difference between any pair of reproductions).

In reproduction No. 2 of the original version a measure of the staccato and disjointed character is clearly discernible. For example, themes h) and k) appear abruptly without any preparation, and themes n), q) and s) are quite disconnected. Nevertheless, the account as a whole is an adequate rendition of the story, though far less so than reproduction No. 2 of the explicated version which is smoother and earns a higher redundancy index (5.69 to 6.64).

There are two prominent gaps in reproduction No. 1 of the original version: between themes q) and s), and between f) and h). It is noteworthy that theme p) stands out from the rest of the text as an essentially unconnected theme: how had he made the discovery that they "were ghosts"? Yet, in spite of its spareness, this is a rather faithful and complete account of the story.

The most complete and accurate of all is reproduction No. 1 of the explicated version which is seventy-eight words longer than its stimulus story, has lost only one theme, and has a redundancy index practically identical with that of its stimulus. It is free of any evident gaps; in fact, it contains a number of importations and amplifications which seem to cement the story further, reducing its minor gaps and further clarifying its ambiguities. It is especially noteworthy that each of the explication themes of the stimulus story is further amplified and embellished in this reproduction. Here we see, in part, a propensity of this particular S; her reproduction of the Secretary story (see below pp. 44-45) is also highly embellished and amplified. In fact, the two reproductions by this S gave rise to the idea of an importation style of remembering, and led me to study this tendency in later experiments.

At this point, the findings of the direct appraisal of the Ghost Story reproductions can be summed up by noting the high correspondence between impressions of the relative coherence and continuity of a reproduction and its redundancy index.[12] In only one case (reproduction No. 3) was the redundancy index not fully compatible with the impression.

SERIAL REPRODUCTIONS OF THE SECRETARY STORY BY THE O-GROUP

REPRODUCTION NO. 1
The War Attacks

a) Two sisters graduated from the same business school. They decided to go abroad to work at embassies; because that way, *b*) they said, "We can work and still see the world." *c*) So they went to neighboring foreign countries. *d*) They agreed to write to each other every day.

g) One sister's secretarial skill got her a job at the ministry of Montania. *f*) The country was in the grip of war hysteria. *h*) The minister told her that she would have access to much top-secret information; he said, "I expect loyalty."

i) One day she came across a document *j*) describing a sneak air attack to be made on a small neighboring nation. *k*) She read it with interest until she noticed the name of the country and *l*) saw with

---

[12] Since the texts differ in lexical content, it is not possible to demonstrate that the extent of the difference in redundancy indexes is traceable in each case to the gaps detected upon direct examination. Nevertheless, my impression of a gap regularly arose where a new lexical element (or group of elements) entered the text unheralded, and when it remained disconnected by virtue of being unrepeated elsewhere in the text. Such unprepared and isolated lexical elements add substantially to the redundancy index of a text, and, in the case of two texts that are equivalent in size and content, it is these elements which make the difference in redundancy.

horror that it was the country where her sister worked. *m*) She immediately wanted to write to her sister and warn her of the danger, but censorship prevailed between the two countries and she could not.

o) She therefore decided to stop writing to her sister. *p*) "If I do not write, she will worry, think I am ill, and come to find out."

q) On the same day that she put her plan into effect, her sister stopped writing to her. *r*) She began to worry and to fear *s*) that her sister was ill *t*) and decided to go and to see her. *u*) Since the distance was only twelve kilometers, she decided that walking would be the *simplest* way. *v*) When she got to the border whom should she meet but her sister, *w*) *and discovered that the other nation was planning a similar attack on her country.*

x) The same day both attacks were carried out and both embassies destroyed.

REPRODUCTION NO. 2

a) Two girls, sisters, graduated from business school and decided to get jobs abroad *b*) so they could "see the world" and "earn while doing so." *c*) They got jobs in adjoining countries in the embassies. *d*) They decided to write each other every day.

g) One girl got a job with the air minister. *h*) He said the job was very important and highly confidential.

i) One day the girl came across a secret document *j*) on the plans for a sneak air attack on a neighboring country—*l*) it was the same one where her sister worked. *n*) *She wanted to save her sister but didn't know how.*

m) All mail was censored. *o*) She finally decided not to write, *p*) then her sister would think she was sick and come to visit her.

q) The day she stopped writing so did her sister. *r*) After a while she became worried about her sister *t*) she decided to walk over to the neighboring country to see her. *u*) It was only twelve kilometers away.

v) When she got to the border who should she see coming toward her but her sister.

x) Both countries attacked the other that day and both embassies were destroyed. *Both sisters were saved because they weren't at their jobs in the embassies.*

REPRODUCTION NO. 3

a) Two girls, sisters, graduated from business school and decided to live and work abroad.

c) They each had a job in an embassy of two adjoining countries. *i*) One sister discovered one day the plans *j*) for a sneak air attack on the adjoining country *l*) where her sister worked.

m) The mail was censored and *n*) she couldn't figure any way to get a warning to her. *o*) She finally decided to stop writing to her *p*) so she would think she was ill and would come to see her. *q*) At the same time the sister in the adjoining country stopped writing also.

r) When she received no mail from her sister she became worried *t*) and decided to walk to the next country to see her. *u*) She walked to the border, *about* twelve kilometers off, *v*) and met her sister coming to her.

x) The next day each country attacked each other and both embassies were destroyed, but both girls were safe, as they were not at work in the embassies.

REPRODUCTION NO. 4

a) Two sisters, *recently* graduated from business school, decided to live in and work in a foreign country.

c) The girls secured positions in two adjoining countries.

i) One girl learned of the plans *j*) of a sneak air attack on *the* adjoining country.

m) She could not write to her sister of this because of *heavily* censored mail, *n*) so wondered how she could warn her sister *of impending disaster.*

o) She decided to stop writing to her sister *p*) *in the hope* that she would be thought ill, and her sister would then come to see her.

q) However, at the same time the sister stopped writing.

r) Concerned for her sister's *safety, t*) she decided to walk to the country where her sister was. *u*) After she had walked toward the border, *approximately* twelve kilometers, *v*) she was met by her sister who had started to walk toward that country.

x) The air attack did occur—many lives *were lost,* but the *sister* was safe because she *was not where she should have been.*

REPRODUCTION NO. 5

a) Two sisters went to business college. They wanted to get jobs in foreign countries.

c) Each got a job in *another* country.

j) One sister heard of a sneak air attack. *m*) She wanted to tell her sister but could not write about it due to heavy censure of mail.

o) She finally decided not to write, *p*) hoping her sister would figure she was ill and come to her.

q) She stopped writing but at the same time she received no letters from her sister.

r) Fearing for the *health* of her sister, *u*) she started walking to see her sister. *v*) She met her sister part of the way *w*) *as she, too, had started to find why mail had stopped coming.*

x) The attack took place—many people were killed, but the girl was safe as she was not where she should have been.

SERIAL REPRODUCTIONS OF THE SECRETARY STORY BY THE E-GROUP

REPRODUCTION NO. 1

The Sneak Attack

a) Two sisters, who had graduated from a business college named Menassa, decided to seek employment in foreign countries. *b*) They told their mother, "In that way we will obtain work and still see the world."

c) So they departed into separate countries. *e*) One sister went to the country of Montania *g*) and because of her excellent stenographic training, was made secretary to the foreign ambassador. *h*) "You will have access to the *most* secret documents," he warned the girl. "I will expect *utmost* loyalty from you," he further told her.

i) One day somewhat later *in the pursuance of her duties* she came across a document *j*) which revealed a plan for attacking, by bombing, a nearby smaller nation. *k*) She read this with considerable interest until, to her horror, she noted the name of the small nation to be bombed. *l*) She discovered it to be the country where her sister was residing.

n) She wondered, *with great fear*, how she could warn her sister of the impending attack *o*) and then thought of the following plan. She would desist from writing her usual daily letter to her sister, *p*) her sister would become alarmed and come to visit her, to see if she were sick or in need of something. *q*) On the *very* day she proceeded to put her plan into operation, the daily letter she usually received from her sister did not arrive. *r*) She noted this with great disturbance and in the days that followed, when no more letters from her sister were forthcoming, *t*) she decided to act.

u) She proceeded toward the border of Montania, which was a distance of twelve kilometers. *v*) *To her amazement*, at the border she met her sister *w*) who was on the way to see her, telling her an identical story.

x) That day both countries were bombed and both embassies were destroyed.

REPRODUCTION NO. 2

a) Two sisters graduated from a business school, Menassa. They decided to take jobs in foreign countries. *b*) They told their mother that in this way they could work and "still see the world." *e*) One sister went to Montania. *g*) Because of her stenographic skill she obtained the job as secretary to the foreign ambassador. *h*) She was told that she would be handling secret documents and that absolute loyalty was expected of her. *i*) One day, in the pursuit of her duties, she came upon a document *j*) which told of plans for an attack on a nearby nation. *k*) She read this plan to bomb the nation with considerable interest until she realized *l*) it pertained to the nation wherein her sister resided. *n*) She tried to think of some way to warn her sister *o*) and finally evolved the following plan: she would not write her customary daily letter to her sister. *p*) Her sister would become alarmed and visit her to see if she were sick. *q*) She did not write the letter but noted with alarm that she did not receive a letter from her sister either. *r*) As the days passed with no word from her sister she became more concerned and *t*) decided to visit her sister. *v*) She met her sister at the border *w*) and the sister told *of a similar plan to bomb Montania*. *x*) Both embassies were destroyed.

REPRODUCTION NO. 3

a) Two girls had graduated from business college—Manessa. They both wanted to be secretaries to foreign ministers. *e*) One of the girls went to Montania *g*) where she became the secretary to the foreign ambassador. Her sister went to another nation. *h*) The first sister was told that she would handle a lot of secret documents and she must keep them absolutely to herself. *i*) One day she came across a plan *j*) to bomb a neighboring country. *k*) As she read it through, *l*) she realized it was her sister's nation. *n*) She tried to think of a plan to let her sister know about the bombing. *o*) She decided not to write her customary letter to her sister *p*) whereupon her sister would become alarmed and come to visit her. *q*) She did not receive a letter from her sister *r*) and became alarmed herself. *v*) She went to meet her sister at the border *w*) and found out that the sister's nation also had made plans to bomb Montania. *x*) Both nations were destroyed.

REPRODUCTION NO. 4

a) Two sisters graduated from *the same* secretarial school—Manessa. Both wanted to obtain jobs as secretaries to foreign ministers. *c*) Both sisters received positions in foreign nations. *g*) The first sister got a job as secretary to the foreign minister in the country Montania. *h*) She was told she would handle many papers which were to be kept secret. *l*) One day she received a paper *j*) which gave information concerning a plan to bomb another nation. *k*) Upon reading it she realized that it was the country in which her sister worked. *n*) She wanted to warn her sister *o*) and decided that, instead of writing her usual letter to her sister, she would not write. *p*) If her sister did not receive the letter, she would come to see her. *q*) The first sister did not receive a letter *r*) and became worried. *v*) She met her sister at the border *w*) and discovered that Montania was to be bombed. *x*) Both nations were destroyed.

REPRODUCTION NO. 5

a) Two sisters went to secretarial school. Both wanted to be secretaries to foreign ministers. *g*) The first sister became secretary to the minister of Montania. *c*) The other sister was in another foreign country. *h*) The first sister was *sworn to secrecy*. *j*) Later she learned a bomb was to be dropped on the country *l*) her sister was in. *She could not break her oath o*) and decided if she did not write, *p*) her sister would come to see what was wrong. *r*) The sister did worry *v*) and met her sister at the border of Montania. *Both were killed.*

Starting again with the ends of the chains, it is noteworthy that the degree of collapse in both reproductions No. 5, though appreciable, is not as great as in those of the Ghost Story. The collapse is more evident in reproduction No. 5 of the E-group than in that of the O-group.[13] The former is more fragmented, contains a few gaps especially from theme *r*) on, and has a noteworthy dis-

---

[13] The superiority of the O-group in their reproductions of the Secretary Story contrasts with the superiority of the E-group in their reproductions of the Ghost Story. It shows that the O-group was superior in recall ability, and thus the difference between the groups in their recall of the Ghost Story must have been due to the explications.

tortion at the end. The latter, on the other hand, though also rather spare and staccato, contains no major gaps, and is a quite faithful and complete account. Their redundancy indexes are almost identical.

Both reproductions No. 4 of the Secretary Story are coherent and complete accounts. In fact, reproductions No. 1, No. 2, No. 3, and No. 4 of both groups seem remarkably coherent in spite of their progressive loss of themes and information units. This impression tends to corroborate the redundancy analysis, which showed that the redundancy indexes of the Secretary Story reproductions vary only within a narrow range (5.73 to 5.01), without any really systematic decreases. The difference between the redundancy indexes of the two No. 4 reproductions, which is the largest of any pair (5.73 to 5.06), is reflected clearly in the texts: the E-group reproduction is conspicuously smoother and more flowing.

Reproduction No. 1 of the O-group presents an especially faithful account of the Secretary Story. In theme w), there is an amplification of the original phrase "for the same reason" into a full-blown explication. This importation of explications is especially conspicuous in reproduction No. 2 of the O-group, where the closing sentence is added to drive home the denouement of the story.

The lead-off member of the E-group—whose account is not as complete as her opposite number's—shows the same tendency to amplify and embellish here that she showed in her reproduction of the Ghost Story. Many of her importations in this case seem more to highlight the events of the story, to furnish emphasis and color, than to provide cohesiveness. (It is as though the familiar content needs no explication.) These importations are, for the most part, unprepared for and unrepeated, and hence they reduce the over-all redundancy of the text. Whereas this S maintained the redundancy level of the Ghost Story in her reproduction of it, in the case of the more familiar Secretary Story she reduced it substantially (6.11 to 5.37). The lead-off member of the O-group, on the other hand, reduced the redundancy of both stories by approximately the same amount (about 0.50).

The Fate of Content in Serial Reproductions

I will now trace certain themes and information units through the serial reproductions of the Ghost Story, paying particular attention to the vicissitudes of the explications in the explicated version chain, and to the gappy and ambiguous parts of the original version. Explications—both those inserted by the experimenter and those that Ss introduced in the course of reproduction—should prove to play a pivotal role in influencing the course of reproductions. In the present analysis I also pay special attention to those parts of the story which dropped out or became the locations of distortions and importations.

Reproduction No. 1 of the original version loses six themes. Three of these were associated with the ambiguities and gaps that I ameliorated in the explicated version. For example, consider the gap between themes b) and d) (I "closed" it in the explicated version by emphasizing the omen): theme c), SOMETHING UP, which I added simply for word count, drops out completely in reproduction No. 1. Following this, the account of the one man's refusal to go and his reason for not going (again a point I had explicated in the explicated version) is condensed into "the two men discussed who should go." Finally, theme p), REALIZATION, is displaced from its original central position in the story and occurs instead at the end with REVELATIONS. Moreover, the account now merely says that "he had discovered that the men . . . were ghosts" and omits the part that suggests how he did so (another of my major explications).

If we compare this reproduction with the lead-off reproduction of the explicated version (it is discussed more fully below), we can appreciate the prominent part played by those gaps and ambiguities in the original version that I had ameliorated. Reproduction No. 1 of the explicated version loses only one theme and that a relatively minor one: REACTION OF THE PEOPLE. On the other hand, reproduction No. 1 of the original version clearly shows the disintegrative influence of the gaps and ambiguities: some of the themes associated with them are lost entirely, others are changed and fragmented in such a way that they cause further fragmentation and loss in subsequent reproductions. For example, the deficiency in handling the ghost element of the story is probably responsible for the conspicuous vicissitudes of this theme in the later reproductions.

In reproduction No. 2 of the original version only one theme is lost and that is theme t), which I had added to the original version merely to equate it to the explicated version; it was not intended to contribute to the text, and, like theme *c*) in its stimulus, proved itself to be expendable. There are, however, a number of changes in this reproduction which seem to "prepare for" or initiate thematic losses and distortions in subsequent reproductions. These are changes in emphasis and order, abbreviations of content, rejuxtapositions of themes, and the like, and will be discussed later. At this point it may be worth noting that this S's tendency to skeletonize leads, in addition to the loss of the peripheral theme *t*), to a change from "hunting for seals" to the more familiar "fishing" (I was prompted to do the same in preparing the explicated version); that the discussion between the men concerning who should go is dropped out completely; and that the REALIZATION is reduced to the statement that "they must have been ghosts." This tendency to render the story in a sparer, leaner, more abbreviated form is worth bearing in mind, for it crops up again and struck me as an important individual propensity that contrasts with importation, perhaps its polar opposite.

Reproduction No. 3 of the original version loses two more themes, each ambiguous and gappy in the original story and made even more so in reproductions No. 1 and No. 2. The ENIGMA theme disappears, leaving a residue in the form of an importation via a noteworthy sequence: in reproduction No. 1, "the man did not feel anything, though told he was hit"; in reproduction No. 2, "the man didn't feel any pain" and "he didn't believe it [that he had been shot] because he couldn't feel anything" (here the theme is distorted—not only does he not feel pain, but he does not believe he was hit); now, in reproduction No. 3 the fact that he does not feel anything is omitted and what remains of the theme is only the new statement, "he didn't believe them." A complete distortion has occurred here with only the rationalized component remaining (it is a kind of explication); the gap has been "closed" at the expense of the ENIGMA theme. Finally, theme *p*) has become utterly unintelligible and disconnected. Now the ghost element, made progressively more ambiguous and disconnected in the previous reproductions, has disappeared from the body of the story and hangs on at the end as an isolated fragment.

Five more themes are lost in reproduction No. 4. Theme *b*), ATMOSPHERE, which was given an explicit significance in the explicated version that it lacks in the original, disappears after being contracted and subordinated in the preceding reproductions: in reproduction No. 2 it occupied minor position in the sentence, "they heard the sound of oars through the fog"; it was retained as "in the fog" in reproduction No. 3; it is now squeezed out completely. This sequence of contraction, subordination, and finally omission seems important because it occurs frequently in the chains. Theme h), WAR-PLANS, drops out in a similar way: in reproduction No. 2, "one man said, 'we are going . . .' "; in reproduction No. 3, "the men were going to attack . . ."—here the "saying" drops out and only the men's intentions are included, but these intentions are apparently superfluous since the narrative proceeds right away to describe the battle; and so it is not surprising that in reproduction No. 4 the statement of plans is absent. Similarly theme s): in reproduction No. 1 it is a clause of another sentence—"when the young man reached home he went ashore, lit a fire," etc. In reproduction No. 2 it is further contracted to "he went home, built a large fire," etc. In reproduction No. 3 it is reduced to "he returned home and told . . ."; since the "fire," the "resting," and the "decision to tell" (the etc.'s) have all dropped out, "home" is left bare (nothing happens there), superfluous, and of only minor significance in the narrative. In reproduction No. 4 it is omitted. Finally, theme u) is squeezed out in a similar way.

The ghost element undergoes further modification in reproduction No. 4 which partly strips it of an incongruity, the "he said." This was incongruous in reproduction No. 3 because the previous sentence had said that "he died." Nevertheless, it still retains ambiguity (i.e., who are the "they" who "must have been ghosts"?) which is resolved in reproduction No. 5, where "they" is changed to "he"—a neat bit of rationalization!

Reproduction No. 5 loses two more themes; the man's DEATH and the sounding of the RETREAT, and in the process furnishes some interesting "case material." Beginning with theme n): in reproduction No. 2, "the Indian has been shot. The man didn't feel any pain" is accurate but disconnected; in No. 3, "the Indian is shot," and the enigma aspect is split away and is mentioned later in the text; in No. 4, "the Indian is shot," now the enigma is nowhere stated, leaving this theme wholly isolated; and so finally in reproduction No. 5 it becomes "they must be Indians"; the RE-

TREAT has been transformed and two themes have fallen by the wayside. In the case of theme y), this is the sequence: reproduction No. 2 tells that he "fell down" and then "he was dead"; No. 3, "he died," and the superfluous falling down is omitted; in No. 4 the death is no longer afforded a separate sentence but becomes "... and dies"; finally in reproduction No. 5 this important theme is left out entirely. It is reasonable to suppose that this loss was caused largely by the earlier mishandling of the ghost element. The statement " 'they must have been ghosts' he said" was tacked on at the end in reproduction No. 3, and in reproduction No. 4 persisted in the disconnected statement "they must have been ghosts." Who says this is a mystery; and indeed, in this account, it appears that somehow the man dies and *then* makes the statement. This contradiction is apparently resolved in reproduction No. 5 by sparing him! It may be that the reason he did not die is that "he must have been a ghost." This is an illuminating sequence of successive opening and closing of gaps, of creating and solving ambiguities, of rationalizing and explicating—processes of schema functioning in recall that seem to merit careful and systematic study.

The serial reproductions of the explicated version contain similar, though fewer, such sequences; there is considerably less thematic loss—a direct result, the evidence attests, of the relative absence of gaps and ambiguities in the stimulus story. In reproduction No. 1 there is only one loss: theme x), the REACTION OF THE PEOPLE, a patently inconsequential part of the story. I have already discussed the fact that this reproduction embellishes the story; at this point it is worth noting that *these amplifications occur at just those points where I had already explicated the text*! For example, in theme c) (an explication) there is a major importation which, while it is largely redundant, solidly links themes b) and c). Similarly, themes i) and j) contain importations that add emphasis and clarity. Finally, a group of importations and changes cluster around themes o) and r). Incidentally, the explication I offered in theme o) of the explicated version is on the face of it not satisfactory. It purports to explain the REALIZATION, but is labored and unclear. Reproduction No. 1 simplifies and distorts it with the sentence "he knew he was not an Indian." The part that follows, however, is quite tortured, and therefore it should not be surprising that the subsequent reproductions show a disturbance at this point.

Reproduction No. 2 loses three more themes, none of which seems essential to the structure of the story.[14] Theme *a*), which tells of the expedition, is changed so that the men simply "were on the beach"; WAR-PLANS is omitted and the two men are merely asked to accompany the men in the canoe; and the ENIGMA is not repeated during the REVELATIONS. The entire character of this reproduction seems to reflect this *S*'s unwillingness to repeat what she has already written. Her stimulus, reproduction No. 1, was a highly elaborated and redundant narrative and it seems that she wants to boil the story down to its essential and nonredundant parts. This attempt, even though it does not entail much loss of accuracy, seems to create gaps and ambiguities that may be responsible for loss of accuracy in the subsequent reproductions.

Reproduction No. 3, while it drops only three more themes, loses considerably in structure and coherence. Theme *c*), SOMETHING UP, drops out after a sequence of progressive contractions: in reproduction No. 1, ". . . night becomes foggy and calm and they knew this denoted . . ."; in reproduction No. 2, ". . . night was foggy and calm—a night on which . . ." (note how the terms "becomes," "knew," and "denoted," which focus attention on what follows, drop out); in reproduction No. 3, ". . . couldn't see anything because of the fog"—here the omen is completely lost. Moreover, "fog" has become subordinate, and is lost in the next reproduction. The other two themes, HIDING and PERMISSION, drop out with apparently no preparation.

Reproductions No. 4 and No. 5 each lose three more themes, although the former theme *a*) reappears, probably because the men are repeatedly called "fishermen" in the previous reproductions and, while they were "sitting on the beach," they might well have been "fishing off shore." In reproduction No. 5, theme *p*) has become disconnected and ambiguous, and it is a reasonable guess that, if there were a reproduction No. 6, we would see either a distortion or a complete deletion of the ghost element.

---

[14] In general, loss of information was greatest for peripheral parts of the story. I did not, however, systematically study this phenomenon; other researchers (e.g., Newman, 1939) have, and found that it could be reliably demonstrated.

General Discussion and Conclusions

Three general findings emerged from the direct examination of the reproductions. (1) Impressions of the quality and structure of the reproductions were congruent with the quantitative indices; particularly important was the correspondence between impressions of over-all coherence or continuity and the redundancy indexes. (2) Some recurring sequences of skeletonization, transformation, and importation were revealed; these may prove to be among the basic schema processes. (3) Certain Ss favored one of these processes—some imported new content and elaborated the story, others stripped away material and pared the story. An important individual differences parameter pertaining to style of remembering may be reflected in these propensities.

In this section I will take up each of these three general findings separately and discuss them at some length by referring to relevant literature and theory. The object is to place the findings in the conceptual framework that directed this program of research.

1. Validity of the Quantitative Indices

Those reproductions which scored lowest in the accuracy and redundancy measures were those which seemed, on direct examination, to be the most fragmented and disconnected: they lacked over-all coherence and failed to convey the core of the story. These impressions confirmed the results of the objective measures —the rapid decline in both accuracy and structure of the original version of the Ghost Story, the less rapid decline of the explicated version, and the least decline of the Secretary Story. The Secretary Story did not undergo a systematic decrease in redundancy index as the others did, and, upon examination, this corresponded to its relatively well-maintained coherence and continuity.

Therefore, by using the three indices together (information unit, theme, and redundancy index) we can appraise a reproduction in terms of how accurately it maintains the information, completeness, and over-all structure of the stimulus story. This appraisal, however, will not be complete. For one thing, the redundancy measure is not ideal for locating and assessing gaps and ambiguities, since it is affected by other factors as well (e.g., a repetitive style of writing will artificially, though not grossly, increase the redundancy index). Moreover, the measure cannot be used to compare texts that differ substantially in content and complexity. What is needed for this purpose is a technique which will analyze the structure of an extended and connected text without being influenced by its particular content and level of complexity. A linguistic method, called Discourse Analysis, has been devised by Zellig Harris (1952, 1954) for just such problems of assessing structure. I have begun some preliminary work with it, have found it promising, and plan to investigate memory data with this tool.

2. The Schema Processes of Explication, Importation, and Skeletonization

The direct examination highlighted the role of explications: they seemed to play an important integrative role in reproductions. Whether experimentally introduced into the Ghost Story or imported by the *S*, explications enhanced continuity by closing gaps, forming transitions, and solving contradictions; they ameliorated ambiguity by transforming the unfamiliar into the familiar, the unlikely into the likely, and so forth. Frequently, explications functioned by anticipating, preparing for, or merely repeating story material and thereby increased the redundancy and coherence of the reproductions.

Lost or distorted themes, traced through the serial reproductions, frequently followed a course of progressive contraction of content together with shifts of interrelationships. In the process of skeletonization, the eventually lost or distorted theme often became secondary and subordinate to another theme. This process resulted in the theme's becoming either redundant or peripheral before it was lost. Gaps were opened and themes became disconnected and isolated. Such gaps were usually closed in one of two ways: (1) by importations of new material (usually explicatory), (2) by the "squeezing out" of old material. That the latter occurred more often is perhaps because in this experiment accuracy was emphasized and lengthy and complex stimulus material was given limited exposure. Nevertheless, the pattern of skeletonization regularly included reshuffling of emphasis, rejuxtaposition of parts and relationships, and a steady tightening of structure around gaps and ambiguities, as well as a stripping away of redundant and ambiguous parts.

Importation, on the whole, occurred less frequently than skeletonization. Though it was not possible in every instance to pin down the function of an importation, usually its explicatory nature was conspicuous—it smoothed gaps, solved ambiguities and contradictions, and enhanced redundancy. Indeed, *only those importations which were patently explicatory went on to influence subsequent reproductions.*

Importation—sometimes called "invention" or "intrusion"—is a regular finding in studies of the retention of extended verbal material[15] and it is usually taken to highlight the functional, rational, and constructive aspects of memory. Davis and Sinha (1950), for example, reported that intrusions play a big part in people's recall of a story after the interpolation of a picture that is relevant to the story. Belbin (1950) similarly reported importations in recall, and showed how they tend to "fill the gaps" in the text. Kirkpatrick (1932) found a good deal of gap-filling when rumors were spread among students. And, under the category of *assimilation,* Allport and Postman (1947) spoke of importations which "fit" and improve the Gestalt of a remembered experience. Importation is related to the difficulty of the stimulus material, at least in children, who invent and substitute more in recalling difficult than simple poetry (Northway, 1940). Northway also found that younger children import more than older ones.

I tentatively conclude, therefore, that importation and its opposite, skeletonization, represent basic processes of schema formation and utilization. These processes can be conceptualized in terms of Hebb's neuropsychological theory (1949), which also provides an appropriate model for the schema concept. Since there may be some important advantages in applying his theoretical model, it will be spelled out here in some detail.

Schema, Phase Sequence, Fractionation, and Recruitment

Hebb attempts a reconciliation and integration of connectionism and configurationism. He begins by proposing that learning (which, in his view, lies at the heart of all psychological functioning) early in the life of an organism differs fundamentally from later learning.

---

[15] Intrusions also occur in the learning of nonconnected material. Deese and Hardman (1954) report that up to two thirds of the errors in paired-associate learning are likely to be intrusions from interpolated material.

Early learning follows association principles mediated by simple connections between the cortical representations of perceptual and motor elements. Once this stage of learning has established circular networks called *cell assemblies*, the organism no longer makes such connections between cortical representations of discrete stimuli; behavior modifications are then accomplished by realignments and repatternings among these cell assemblies. But Hebb does not imply a simple trace theory even for this first stage of learning. Experience at no point becomes internalized by an automatic isomorphic process; rather, from the very first it becomes internalized in an essentially schemalike way. The theory specifies the way this schema formation might conceivably occur.

The first misconception to discard, Hebb says, is the idea of a passive brain which requires external excitation to activate it. There is considerable evidence that the cortex is largely self-activating and that nerve cells frequently fire spontaneously. This means that sensory excitation feeds into an already active cortex. A repeated pattern of stimulation, according to Hebb, can slowly gain control over the spontaneous firing and give rise to widespread reverberating circuits that will subsequently be triggered by this pattern of stimulation. In this way simple and repeated experience gradually results in the formation of rudimentary reverberatory cell networks—the cell assemblies.

These structures are fundamentally like concepts. For example, the superordinate cell assembly which corresponds to the perception of a triangle is the product of stimulations by a variety of different-sized and -colored triangles from various angles and in various perspectives. Hebb describes the process by which, in the course of the development of the cell assembly, the neural correlates of irregular or sporadic stimulations are stripped away until finally only those which correspond to the invariant common features of *triangle* remain: the cell assembly then represents the concept triangle. Two processes are responsible for forming the cell assembly in this way: *fractionation* and *recruitment*. The former refers to the stripping away or the weakening of those connections and networks that are only sporadically reinforced (the variable aspects of the stimulation); the latter refers to the strengthening or facilitation of recurring aspects of the stimulation (the commonality of the stimulation).

Once cell assemblies reach a certain stage of development they become relatively closed and relatively autonomous. That is, they become relatively independent from sensory excitation, and are capable of spontaneous firing due to intracerebral metabolic conditions, or triggered by other cell assemblies. From this point on, a new kind of integration becomes the rule: cell assemblies link themselves together into higher-order temporal-spatial organizations. Such linkages—Hebb calls them phase sequence—differ fundamentally from the relatively permanent binding that formed the cell assembly.

The phase sequence is a temporally extended, relatively flexible, complex integration of widespread cell assemblies. Hebb stresses the relative autonomy of these central structures—their growing independence from external stimulation, their growing dependence on internal conditions (especially on the neural correlates of need, motivation, and emotion) and on the activity of other structures, and their ability to be self-triggering. Most important, in relation to stimulation they are essentially conceptlike—abstractive and skeletal. Fractionation and recruitment continue as basic processes in phase-sequence development and operation. The former refers to the stripping away (by short-circuit mechanisms) of cell assemblies, the latter to the incorporation of new assemblies.

The phase sequence has most of the properties that have been assigned to the schema. Like the schema, it is an internalized, relatively autonomous, potentially self-active, conceptual representation of experience which at once grows out of experience and is the basis for experience.

The schema processes that were inferred from direct examination of the serial reproductions in the present study centered on the two ways in which gaps and ambiguities were solved: by importation and skeletonization. The former may be considered a behavior correlate of recruitment, the latter of fractionation. The correspondence between the phenomena and the concepts may, in a strict sense, be crude; nonetheless it is striking and provocative.

I propose that the system that forms the basis for learning and retaining an extended and connected experience, such as a story, is not a rigidly bound, passive, and static structure. Rather it is a temporally integrated group of widespread and relatively autonomous cortical organizations—schemas. In order to execute a reproduction of the story, this temporally extended pattern is "run off." It must be assumed that this "running off" will partly reflect the manner in which the organization was originally formed, and two basic processes which they share are fractionation and recruitment.

His use of such concepts as schema and phase sequence reflects, I believe, a theorist's willingness to place greater emphasis on the *emitted* nature of behavior, on the lack of uniform correlations between stimuli and responses, and on the importance of relatively autonomous structures, conceived as internal to the organism, which arise as a product of the organism's history in commerce with its environment. Such structural concepts can be applied to all aspects and modes of cognition (memory is certainly continuous with perception and learning). For example, following Woodworth's formulation (1938, pp. 73-77), perception can be conceived of as schema "with correction," and the role of external stimulation can be understood as the facilitation, control, and steering of cognitive behavior rather than as the direct determination (stimulation) of response.

This view is supported by a variety of sources, and such studies as the one reported by Granit (1921) provide basic evidence. He found that children do not remember a figure unless they find it similar to a familiar object. Furthermore, children apparently do not conceive of the figure as being formed by lines—they are objects. Granit concluded that the child draws a schema of what he knows about the figure and not what he sees. Of course, we would have to take it further and argue that "what he sees" is in fact determined largely by "what he knows" about the stimulus.

There is a trap in this line of thinking—the trap of solipsism and tautology—if it is not realized that such a formulation is necessarily a first approximation, and must eventually be followed by careful specifications and definitions. But these specifications and definitions can open the problem up rather than prematurely stifle it. One can take the same position as Wolters (1933), who writes: ". . . the schemata can only be deduced from the actual behavior, but probably we should conceive of them as existing continuously, as characters of the organism, but not as entities which the organism 'possesses' " (p. 136). Wolters shows that schemas are the means of thinking rather than the objects of thought, using as an example the way we use numbers in mathematical thinking. The fact that we are also able to think about the particular numbers means, to Wolters, that the organism can somehow "turn round upon, or react to, *itself as schematized*." Wolters, incidentally, presents a definition of schema that is identical to McDougall's famous definition of instinct (". . . an innate psychophysical disposition which determines its possessor to perceive, and to pay attention to, objects of a certain class, . . . and to act in regard to [them] in a particular manner."), except that the term "innate" is omitted.

3. *Individual Differences in Remembering: Importing and Skeletonizing as Cognitive Styles*

Individual differences in recall can be demonstrated, according to Gomulicki (1956, p. 400), ". . . with a degree of statistical significance that makes it perilous to ignore them when designing experiments in recall." The differences he refers to are of ability as well as quality and manner of recall. The high price of ignoring individual differences is illustrated by the confusion in the literature regarding the influence of affective and motivational factors on cognition.

Though it is now generally accepted that such relationships and influences exist and are important (especially for an understanding of everyday learning and retention), many experiments still fail to discover any influence of needs and affects upon retention—for example, see Williams (1950). There seems to be an element of "now you see it, now you don't" in the phenomena.

Rapaport (1942), reviewing the experiments on the influence of emotions on memory, suggested that the reason for the fickleness of the phenomena is that experimenters usually overlook a central component of the relationship: the subject's stable and enduring features which mediate between motivation and cognition.[16] Klein (1954) supports this point of view, and has effectively demonstrated the mediating and directing role of cognitive styles (sometimes called "system principles") in the relationship between need and perception. The subject's style can sometimes determine in which of two opposite ways he will react to frustration and deprivation, for example. When groups of subjects are studied and their reactions are pooled, such interactions may be completely obscured

---

[16] Rapaport (1957) has recently presented a thorough discussion of this point.

and any systematic influences of motivations and affects become obliterated.

The exploration of the influence of motivation on retention therefore requires a systematic study of mediating structures by means of a study of individual differences. If there are in fact styles of remembering, they must be studied and implicated in any research on memory. The concept of style refers to the extended mode of operation of a schema organization, and embraces such properties as its complexity, stability, and temporal-sequential patterning. A new parameter can be added to this list, fractionation and recruitment, which may embrace an important dimension of cognitive style and hence point the way to a basic area of individual differences.

I decided to study this parameter, and began by hypothesizing that a style dimension is implicit here, one which can be described as a propensity to import and elaborate versus a tendency to skeletonize and fragment. Individuals in whom the recruiting process is particularly pronounced will make importations to a greater extent than those in whom the fractionating process is dominant.

A series of experimental questions immediately arose: can groups of Ss be distinguished with respect to this tendency? Is it a stable aspect of an individual's performance on retention tasks? Will the fate of stories recalled by groups of importers and skeletonizers be different? Will explication and familiarity exert different effects upon such groups? These questions form the basis of the experiments which are presented in the following chapter.

3

RETENTION STYLE AND RETENTION ABILITY

The closing discussion section of Chapter 2 focused on the complementary processes of recruitment and fractionation—whose empirical correlates are importation and skeletonization—and raised some questions about their roles in schema formation and function. The present chapter reports three interlocking experiments designed to answer the following questions pertaining to them: (a) Can groups of Ss be distinguished with respect to these propensities? (b) Do they represent stable properties of an individual's performance on retention tasks, i.e., cognitive styles? (c) Will these contrasting styles be reflected by the divergent fates of stories passed serially through groups of importers and nonimporters? (d) Will explication and familiarity have different effects upon such groups of Ss?

Experiment I was designed for two purposes: (1) to answer questions (a) and (b) about individual differences; and, if the answer was positive (as it was), (2) to permit the selection of separate groups of Ss, each homogeneous with respect to retention ability and style, to form into serial reproduction chains which would then yield data pertaining to questions (c) and (d). Experiment II consisted of the serial transmission of explicated and original versions of stories through these groups of Ss. Experiment III—an integration and replication of the foregoing experiments with a fresh group of Ss—consisted of the serial transmission of the Ghost Story (in its original and explicated versions) and the Secretary Story through chains of good retainers who were grouped into importers and nonimporters.

Experiment I: Individual Differences in Retention Ability and Importation

Purpose

The major purpose of the first experiment was to explore systematically the subject variables *ability* and *style*, to find out whether they do in fact represent stable individual differences which can be reliably measured. My original purpose was to devote as much study to skeletonization as to importation, having conceived of them as opposites along a single continuum. However, after preliminary exploration and analysis, difficulties arose with respect to the assessment of skeletonization. As a result, the major emphasis was limited to importation versus nonimportation. Study of the data also led me to explore another variable: the use and retention of imagery.

Methods and Procedures

ASSESSING RETENTION STYLES

A technique for assessing importation and skeletonization should evoke and enhance these tendencies and provide for their easy measurement. To this end, I devised a procedure modeled on retroactive interference: The S first learns a set of verbal statements, next he performs an independent though related verbal task, and then he recalls the original set of statements. This recall is examined both for importations—the infiltration of material from the intervening task—and for evidence of skeletonization.

The technique in detail is as follows. A list of seven sentences was prepared, each a terse statement of one of the seven major themes of an Indian folk tale called "The Balanced Rock." S's first task is to learn this list of themes. His next task is to make up a story based upon the theme list (the instructions urge him to use different words and try to compose a good story). Finally, S is asked to reproduce the original theme list (the instructions urge word-perfect accuracy).

The assumption underlying this technique is that a comparison between the original theme list, S's story (his *composition*), and his reproduction of the theme list will yield a valid and reliable index of his tendency to import. We can observe what new information appears in the reproduction of the theme list and see whether this new material is derived from the composition. Furthermore, since the original theme list was already skeletonized, Ss who tend to skeletonize and fragment can be expected to make their reproduction even briefer and more terse than the original.

This is the theme list:

THEME LIST FOR THE STORY "THE BALANCED ROCK"

Theme 1: Indian boys /[1] are playing / at testing / their strength. /
Theme 2: The winner / is vain / and boastful. /
Theme 3: A strange lad / appears / who is mocked / and challenged. /
Theme 4: The stranger / wins / every feat. /
Theme 5: He turns into / the / Stone Giant. /
Theme 6: The boys / are reprimanded / and shamed. /
Theme 7: He turns into / a rabbit. /

The instructions for learning the theme list were:

I am passing out a sheet which contains a list of themes of a story called "Balanced Rock." I would like you to read this list of themes carefully and get to know them. Read the list through three or four times. When you are through, turn this sheet face down and look up. Please go ahead now, read the list carefully three or four times and get to know it.

After the sheets were collected, the instructions to compose a story were given:

Now I would like each of you to compose a story which is based on the theme list you just studied. That is, *in your own words*, write out the story. Add things as you wish—make it a good story-narrative based on the list of themes. Make it about 150 words long, and take at least ten minutes to do it in. Any questions? Do you all understand what I want you to do? Remember: about 150 words and try to write at your usual writing pace. This is not a test of you, or anything like that, but do a good job anyway. When you finish, read your composition through once.

[1] The crossbars mark off the information units; they were not shown on the stimulus copies.

After the compositions were handed in, reproductions of the theme list were requested:

> Now I would like for you to write out, as accurately as you can recall, the theme list which was on that sheet—the list of themes that you read three or four times. Try to be as precise as you possibly can in reproducing what was on that sheet. Any questions? Remember, be as precise as you can.

ASSESSING RETENTION ABILITY

I expected that individuals would differ not only in style of recall, but in the efficiency with which they learn, retain, and reproduce.[2] Aside from being itself of some interest, such a factor must be controlled in order to isolate the style variable (to separate the *how* from the *how well*) and to study the effects of explication and familiarity. Therefore, some way to assess S's retention ability was needed.

The theme-list technique, described above, in addition to measuring importation and skeletonization, can also measure accuracy. However, this measure may not be a pure one since it will probably be contaminated by the interpolated task. Therefore, to assess retention ability I used a straightforward story retention task, employing the method of successively repeated reproductions, which requires S to give several reproductions of a stimulus at various time intervals from the original exposure.[3] An interval of approximately fifteen minutes (filled with an unrelated concentration task) was interposed between the initial learning and the first reproduction.

For the test of retention ability, I selected a Korean tale titled "The Bedbug, Louse, and Flea" (called here the Bedbug Story).

---

[2] Is there a generalized learning factor? Even though recent studies (e.g., Woodrow, 1940) have found low correlations among learning tasks, nevertheless in such tasks as serial-list learning the ability of Ss has proved to be an important parameter (slow learners recall better after massed practice and fast learners after spaced practice [Estes, 1956]). The failure of researchers to uncover individual differences in recall may be due to their failure to distinguish between the retention of detail and the retention of meaning, or what has been called "substance" memory. In the latter category Winch (1911) reported substantial individual differences.

[3] This method has occasioned a good deal of controversy concerning both the so-called "trace fate" issue (see Woodworth [1938], Hanawalt [1937], Hebb and Foord [1945]) and the phenomenon of "reminiscence" (see Estes [1956]). The essential point is that it has frequently been overlooked that each of the reproductions may serve as an additional learning trial.

It is approximately the same length as the Ghost and Secretary Stories. Although its events have an unfamiliar ring, it does not have gaps and ambiguities of the sort that the original version of the Ghost Story has.

In addition to being measured for retention ability, the reproductions of this story were also examined for the presence of importations. These reproductions along with the theme-list results supplied independent measures of style as well as of ability.

The instructions for learning and reproducing the Bedbug Story were the same as those used for the Ghost and Secretary Stories in the Exploratory Experiment.

The Bedbug Story

The Bedbug, / Louse, / and Flea

a) Long, long ago / a bedbug / reached the age / of sixty, / *b*) and to celebrate / the occasion / held the customary / party, / known as Hwangab, / that marks / the completion / of a whole / sexagenary / cycle. / *c*) He invited / his two / closest / friends, / a louse / and a flea. /

d) The louse / and the flea / set out together / to go to / the party. / *e*) The sprightly / flea / leapt ahead / without regard / for the louse / and before long / had left him far behind. / *f*) The louse / could not walk very fast, / for he was a portly / creature, / and his legs / were very short. / *g*) So he shouted / to the flea, / "Wait for me, / my friend!" /

h) So the flea / walked a little slower / for a time, / *i*) but before long / he lost patience / with the tardy / louse, / for by now / he was feeling rather hungry. / *j*) So he ran / straight / to the bedbug's / house. / *k*) The tables / were heavily laden / with delicious / food / and drink, / *l*) so the flea / said to / the bedbug, / "I am very thirsty, / please let me have a bowl / of wine." / *m*) So the bedbug / filled a bowl / with wine. / *n*) Then / he went out to meet / the louse / on the way. /

o) While the flea / waited for them to arrive / he refilled / his bowl / several times / from the bottles / on the table, / and soon / got very red / in the face. / *p*) When the bedbug / arrived at last / with the louse / the flea / was quite drunk / and was humming / a tune. / *q*) All / the bottles / were empty. / *r*) The louse / was already / annoyed / at the flea's behavior, / and now / he lost his temper / completely / and slapped / his face. / *s*) Then /

there was a rumpus indeed. / The flea / and the louse / grappled / fiercely with one another. / *t*) Their host, / the bedbug, / tried to get between them / to part them, / but they fought on / *u*) and in the end / fell / on top of him, / so that he was squashed / quite flat. /

v) So to this day / the bedbug / is still / a flat / creature, / *w*) the flea / has a tipsy / red face, / *x*) and the louse / has a mark / on his back / where the flea / kicked him. /

CONDUCT OF THE EXPERIMENT

The senior class of a private preparatory school, fifty boys ranging in age from fifteen to sixteen and a half, served as *S*s.[4] The experiment was conducted in three sessions.

Session I: In the initial session the *S*s as a group were given the Bedbug Story and the theme-list task. They were administered in one sixty-minute period in the following sequence: (1) the Bedbug Story was administered; (2) the theme list was administered; (3) the composition based on the theme list was written; (4) the Bedbug Story was reproduced; (5) the theme list was reproduced; (6) the composition was reproduced. Almost twenty minutes elapsed between steps (1) and (4), and between steps (2) and (5). Since it intermeshed the two tasks, the experimental procedure probably invited retroactive and proactive interference, thereby probably maximizing the possibilities of importation and skeletonization, though possibly more the former.

The experiment was not conducted as if it were an examination; the atmosphere seemed more like a class in English Composition. The boys appeared to apply themselves earnestly, and the procedure went smoothly.[5] Some of the boys later commented that they enjoyed the experience although the task of reproducing their own story at the end (step 6) was an arduous one.

Sessions II and III: At no point during sessions I and II were *S*s told that at a future date they would be asked for further recall

---

[4] The mean I.Q. of these boys was above average. On Form B of the Otis Self-Administering Tests of Mental Ability, Higher Examination, their I.Q.s ranged from 95 and 145 (*mean* of 115, *mode* between 120 and 125).

[5] The problem of individual differences in time taken for the various tasks was handled in the following way. When I observed that a majority of the *S*s were finished, I made a short statement pressing the others to finish up as quickly as they could. It frequently happened, however, that several boys were still working when all of the others were through. At such a time I made a second announcement urging those few to finish up quickly.

of the material. Nevertheless, they were asked for reproductions fourteen days after session I and again forty-nine days after that. In this way reproductions of all the experimental material were obtained on three separate occasions: approximately twenty minutes following exposure to the stimulus, fourteen days later, and sixty-three days later. One S was absent at session II, and four more were unable to attend session III. Therefore the data reported in Experiment I are based on an N of 45.

During these sessions the Ss, in spite of some complaining and joking, continued to be interested and cooperative. The following is the order in which reproductions were obtained during sessions II and III and the instructions used to obtain them:

1. The theme list

You recall that list of themes upon which you composed a story? Please write out, as best as you can right now, that list. Remember, this is not a test of you, so don't worry about it too much. But try to do the best you can. Any questions?

2. The Bedbug Story

Thanks. Now you recall you wrote a story based on those themes. But you dealt also with *another* story, one which was typed out, which you read through and later reproduced. That is the story I want you now to reproduce for me to the best of your present ability. Do you all have a clear picture of which story it is I want you to work on? [They all did.] Fine, then go ahead. Try to write at your normal writing speed, don't stop for long periods trying to recollect something, go right on and come back to these points later on.

3. The composition

Now the final thing I want you to do is to reproduce the story which you yourself wrote.

The final step took place six days after session III, when a questionnaire was distributed to all Ss. In addition to a number of general questions about various aspects of the experimental procedure, the questionnaire consisted of a multiple-choice recognition test on the Bedbug Story. It contained twenty-five questions: eighteen asked for a detailed fact of the story, and seven asked for recognition of a particular imagery word or phrase.

Treatment of the Data

MEASUREMENT OF RETENTION ABILITY

The following three measures were used as indices of retention ability:

1. *Theme score:* The theme score represents (as it did in the Exploratory Experiment) the number of correctly reproduced themes. Theme scores were obtained of the Bedbug reproductions, as well as of composition reproductions (the latter were computed as a percentage based on the number of themes contained in the composition itself).

2. *Theme-list score:* Each of the S's three theme-list reproductions was scored at the information-unit level in the following way: each word-perfect replica of an information unit was given 3 points; 2 points went to a unit which was roughly equivalent; and 1 point to one which had some measure of comparability to the original. A bonus of 5 points was given when the reproduction was complete (seven themes).

3. *Questionnaire score:* The sum of the number of correct choices.

I extracted from each composition a fourth index—called an integration score—which may, at least partly, reflect an ability. The extent to which an S can use all seven themes in his composition might be considered an ability variable. To get an estimate of this variable I assessed each composition for the degree to which it integrated or assimilated the original themes, scoring 1 point wherever an information unit of the theme list was accurately mentioned and in some way used in the composition. (I made no attempt to judge the extent to which each unit was successfully or inventively organized into a good story.) The sum of these scores is called the integration score.

MEASUREMENT OF RETENTION STYLES

I derived indices of importation from two sources:

1. *Theme importation:* I counted the number of new themes (i.e., those with no direct counterpart in the stimulus story) in each of the Bedbug Story reproductions as well as in the composition reproductions. I paid no attention to the extent to which a new

theme might have been related to some part of the stimulus material (i.e., how extraneous it was).

2. *Theme-list importation:* Importation of information units into the three theme-list reproductions was assessed by noting those units which were original to the reproduction. These importations were assessed in two ways: in an initial analysis I simply counted them; in a second analysis I made a subjective judgment about the magnitude of the importation (including how extraneous it was). A "major" importation was scored 2, a "minor" importation scored 1, and the total was the importation score for each reproduction.

I found that importations were quite easy to identify and to assess. The Bedbug Story reproductions contained many parts which were patently importations, and, in the case of the theme list, most of them could be traced to the composition that intervened between learning and reproduction. However, my attempt to assess skeletonization encountered difficulties. One source of difficulty lay in the fact that I felt a distinction needed to be made between an omission of a theme and a fragmentation of a theme independent of theme loss. I had anticipated that skeletonization could be detected in a reduction of information units per theme, without loss of theme.

However, the findings did not permit such a distinction. Omission and diminution seemed, for the most part, to overlap, and unmistakable fragmentations of the themes were quite rare—not nearly as common as importations of new information units and themes.

These difficulties of assessment, and the fact that a simultaneous study of four variables (importation, ability, explication, and familiarity) already complicated the experimental design, led me to abandon a systematic study of skeletonization in the present series of experiments. Nevertheless, it was possible to select a few Ss whose theme-list reproductions were conspicuously fragmented. They were formed into a serial reproduction group in Experiment II, and were studied separately.

I also explored the use and retention of imagery. On examining the reproductions, I was struck by the fact that certain Ss reproduced many of the vivid and colorful words and expressions of the Bedbug Story, while other Ss leveled the imagery to simple narrative. Moreover, some Ss used vivid imagery in their compositions and others did not. Therefore, I decided to explore this tendency to see whether it was a stable and independent one. I studied the Bedbug Story and labeled certain words as "imagery words." Then I examined each reproduction of the Bedbug Story for the presence of these words, counted them up, and labeled their sum the *imagery score*. I did the same for each composition as well.

Results

The results of the various measurements are less interesting than those intercorrelations among them which can reveal the presence or absence of stable individual differences in ability and style. Nevertheless, Table 4, which presents the *means* and *standard deviations* of all of the quantitative measures,[6] contains a number of findings that are important in their own right and need to be examined before their intercorrelations can be evaluated. These findings are of two kinds: those that point up the differences between serial reproductions and repeated reproductions; and those that point up a relationship between coherence of stimulus and accuracy of reproductions.

The word count and theme count of the Bedbug Story and the composition reproductions[7] reveal that the loss of material from the first to the third repeated reproductions was surprisingly small compared to the sizable loss which regularly occurs in the same number of serial reproductions. In the repeated reproductions, a majority of Ss showed a steady, though comparatively small loss, while a noteworthy minority, about 30 per cent, showed some gain. It is also worth noting that the differences between reproductions II and III were, on the whole, smaller than between I and II. This difference in loss is more conspicuous in the accuracy measures, particularly of the theme-list reproductions.

These findings highlight the difference between the methods of repeated and serial reproduction. Why does the latter wreak such havoc with stimulus material, while the former shows remarkable

---

[6] Frequency distributions of each of the measures reported in Table 4 were prepared, and they closely approximated the normal distribution.

[7] It is noteworthy that the group complied with the instructions to write a composition of about 150 words. Only three Ss wrote stories shorter than 120 words, and none wrote less than 90. On the other hand, fifteen Ss wrote stories that exceed 200 words. The average story consisted of 16.5 themes; the smallest number of themes in any composition was 9, the greatest, 25.

Table 4

SELECTION DATA FROM EXPERIMENT I

Productivity

a. Original Compositions: Word Count 179.5*(43.5);
   Theme Count 16.5 (3.77)

b. Repeated Reproductions: Word Count

Bedbug I	235.8 (36.9)	Composition I	153.6 (45.3)
Bedbug II	220.7 (45.5)	Composition II	144.4 (47.4)
Bedbug III	213.2 (58.7)	Composition III	137.0 (57.3)

Theme Count

Bedbug I	22.2 (2.23)	Composition I	15.3 (4.02)
Bedbug II	21.3 (3.33)	Composition II	14.3 (3.71)
Bedbug III	20.8 (4.11)	Composition III	14.5 (4.75)

Accuracy

a. Repeated Reproductions: Theme Score

Bedbug I	21.4 (3.76)	Theme List I	26.2 (7.29)
Bedbug II	20.0 (3.69)	Theme List II	20.7 (8.13)
Bedbug III	19.2 (4.02)	Theme List III	19.4 (8.04)
Total	60.6 (9.04)	Total	66.3 (21.8)

b. Theme Loss of the Three Composition Reproductions 19.4% (12.51)

c. Questionnaire Score 18.2 (2.8)

Style

a. Imagery Count: Original Compositions   4.53 (3.66)
   Three Bedbug Reproductions   13.27 (4.87)

b. Importation Score: Three Theme List
   Reproductions   13.84 (6.18)
   Three Bedbug Reproductions   7.29 (4.29)
   Three Composition Reproductions   3.91 (2.71)

* Each entry is a mean based on an N of 45, its standard deviation is in parentheses.

stability? One possible answer is that, in repeated reproduction, retention is affected by unique factors, among which reminiscence and relearning at each reproduction may be the most important. These renewed contacts with stimulus material undoubtedly go far in stabilizing the structure of schema. On the other hand, the serial reproduction method not only limits each individual's contact with the stimulus but also requires that he make sense out of it at each successive step. That the structure of stimulus material is better maintained when repeated reproductions are permitted is an unequivocal conclusion.

In the course of the three reproductions, Ss lost an average of 20 per cent of the themes from their own compositions, whereas they only lost 16 per cent of the themes in the Bedbug Story. Though this difference falls short of statistical significance, the opposite result can be predicted on the basis of the fact that not only did each S have more exposure to his own story, but his own story was on the average considerably shorter than the Bedbug Story. The explanation for this finding may be that the Bedbug Story was a more coherently organized as well as a more vivid stimulus, and hence created a more solid and cohesive schema.[8]

To explore the possible relation between coherence of structure and retention, I made the following analysis of the composition data. Without prior knowledge of how it fared in reproduction, I examined each of the original compositions for its over-all coherence and judged, on an impressionistic and quasi-literary basis, whether it had a "loose" or a "tight" construction. I then compared the mean integration score and mean percentage of theme loss of the "loose" and "tight" compositions.

These results are presented in Table 5. The "tight" group reproduced their compositions better than the "loose" group and also attained higher integration scores. Furthermore, there was a significant inverse relationship between integration scores and percentage of theme loss—for the entire population $r = -.33$. It is apparent that structural coherence and the degree to which the theme list is assimilated are both related to retention, and also related to each other. An S who used most of the theme list and

---

[8] The factor of fatigue, however, cannot be ruled out, since in all of the sessions the composition was reproduced last.

Table 5

THEME LOSS IN REPEATED REPRODUCTIONS
AND INTEGRATION SCORE OF
"TIGHT" AND "LOOSE" COMPOSITIONS

	% Theme Loss		Integration Score	
	"Tight"	"Loose"	"Tight"	"Loose"
Number of Ss	24	15	24	15
Mean	14	26	17.8	15.6
Standard Deviation	10	12	2.4	3.2
Difference between means	t = 3.27, P < .01		t = 2.58, P < .02	

wrote a compact story retained it better than one who either used less of the theme list or organized it into a loose story.

A CORRELATIONAL STUDY OF ABILITY AND STYLE

Now we turn to the main analysis of the data summarized in Table 4: a study of the intercorrelations between the various measures which will test the presence and extent of individual differences in ability and style.

1. *Retention ability:* Eight product-moment correlation coefficients were computed among the accuracy measures of the various tests and reproductions. They are all positive, significantly greater than zero, and rather substantial. Correlations of +.44, +.44, and +.37 for the three reproductions respectively were obtained between the theme score of the Bedbug Story and the theme-list score. The total theme score (across the three reproductions) of the Bedbug Story correlated +.63 with the total number of themes correctly reproduced of the compositions. The total theme-list score correlated +.50 with the questionnaire score.

The integration score of the original composition correlated with both the theme-list score of the first session and the total theme-list score: the r's are $+.59$ and $+.57$ respectively. These two correlations, however, probably reflect more than simple retention ability; they also reflect the finding that the extent to which S was able to integrate the theme list into his story was positively related to his ability to reproduce the theme list. By being used and rehearsed in the composition, the information of the theme list was organized into a coherent schema.

This group of unanimous significant positive correlations, along with the fact that retention ability subsequently held up throughout Experiments II and III, speaks strongly for the presence of an ability factor in the reproduction of such material as stories and lists of related themes.

2. *Importation tendency:* Three correlation coefficients were computed to test whether Ss who imported in one task also imported in the others: they are each positive, significant, and quite substantial. The total number of importations in the three reproductions of the Bedbug Story correlated $+.52$ with the total number of importations in the reproductions of the composition. The importation score derived from the three theme-list reproductions correlated $+.62$ with the importations in the Bedbug reproductions, and $+.45$ with the importations in the composition reproductions.

These correlations attest to an importing tendency that cut across the various retention tasks used in this experiment. Experiments II and III also gave strong testimony to the stability and generality of this tendency to import.

Is this tendency independent of retention ability? The present data revealed no correlation between them. In the course of selecting Ss for the serial-reproduction groups of Experiment II, I carried out a number of further analyses of the present data and analyzed the accuracy and importation of the Bedbug reproductions at the information-unit level. These analyses showed, among other things, that there was no significant correlation between importation tendency and retention ability. These further analyses will be presented and discussed below when the selection procedures for Experiment II are described.

3. *Use and retention of imagery:* Ss used an average of only 4.5 imagery words in their compositions, whereas they reproduced, in their first reproductions, an average of 5.8 of the 18 imagery words of the Bedbug Story. In both their use and retention of imagery words Ss showed individual consistency: the imagery count derived from the original composition correlated $+.60$ with the imagery score from the Bedbug reproductions.

There was also, however, a substantial positive correlation between the imagery and accuracy scores—the imagery score of the Bedbug reproductions correlated $+.50$ with the theme score of that story, and $+.59$ with the percentage of correct themes of the composition. This indicates that retention of imagery words went along with retention ability in general; the good retainers used and retained imagery more than did the poor retainers. On the other hand, they imported neither more or less.

4. *Productivity:* The correlations among the various measures of productivity are of some interest since they attest to the task specificity of reproducing. A comparison between the size of the first Bedbug reproduction and the original composition yielded small and statistically insignificant correlations: in word count, $r = +.18$; in theme count, $r = +.04$. For the second and third reproductions, however, the correlations between the size of the Bedbug reproductions and the compositions became significantly positive: they are $+.45$, $+.42$, $+.48$, and $+.48$. In view of the fact that these four significant correlations apply to a mnemonic task, while the former nonsignificant ones do not, these results indicate that when *S remembers* a good deal of the Bedbug Story, he is also likely to *remember* a good deal of his own composition. But remembering a good deal of the Bedbug Story does not insure the production of a long composition—these tasks are dissimilar, and, according to the correlations, quite independent.

Finally, individual consistency with regard to the size of the reproductions was revealed by the following: the word count of the Bedbug reproduction No. 1 correlated $+.83$ with the word count of the Bedbug reproduction No. 2. Similarly, $r = +.47$ for the theme counts. Moreover, the word count of the composition correlated $+.84$ with the word count of the first reproduction of the composition, and, for the theme counts, $r = +.93$.

Summary and Conclusions

The main purpose of this experiment was to ascertain whether there are significant individual differences in ability and style of retention. The experiment used a number of techniques, including the learning and repeated reproduction of a story, the learning and repeated reproduction of a connected but terse list of themes, the composing of a story based on this list, and the repeated reproduction of this composition.

These methods, singly and in combination, showed the presence of an ability variable and two style variables. All of the measures of accuracy, efficiency, importation, and imagery were substantially and positively correlated. The indices of accuracy, whether of themes or of the more molecular information units, were highly intercorrelated, attesting to the presence of a relatively stable retention-ability variable that cut across the experimental asks. The indices of importation, also at both the level of themes and information units, were highly intercorrelated, indicating that an S who imported in his theme-list reproductions was also likely to import in his repeated reproductions of the Bedbug Story and of his composition. While there was no correlation between retention ability and importation, there was a positive correlation between retention ability and the tendency to use and retain imagery words —which also proved to be a source of consistent individual differences.

In addition to these results on individual differences, the experiment also showed that the degree of coherence of a text seems to be related to subsequent reproduction of it. Ss reproduced the Bedbug Story better than they did their own compositions, and this may have been because of its greater coherence and vividness. Furthermore, those compositions which best integrated or assimilated the theme list were best recalled, and the "tight" ones were subsequently better recalled than the "loose" ones.

An additional finding was that, in a period of over two months, remarkably few themes were lost in these repeated reproductions. This finding contrasts quite sharply with the results of serial reproduction, and shows how strong a stabilizing or structuralizing effect a repeated contact with a stimulus can have.

After Experiments II and III of this series have been presented, all of the conclusions will be drawn together and some of the theoretical issues and concepts that I have already discussed will be joined with them. Experiment I can briefly be summed up as follows. Three relatively independent variables emerged: importing style, retention ability, and text coherence. The first may be especially relevant to the concept of recruitment as a process of schema formation and operation; the second and third may be related to the processes underlying schema structuralization and stability, the one approached from the subject side, the other from the stimulus side.

They have been isolated; their consistency, generality, and interdependence have been assessed. The next step is to pursue the study of these variables with the technique that magnifies forgetting and distortion, while teasing out the threads of process and function—namely, serial reproduction.

EXPERIMENT II: IMPORTING IN RELATION TO RETENTION ABILITY AND EXPLICATION

Purpose

One of the goals of Experiment I was to provide information for arranging a population of Ss into chains for the serial reproduction of original and explicated versions of stories. The present experiment applies the magnifying glass of the serial reproduction technique to two of the variables that were isolated in the preceding experiment: importation tendency and retention ability. These two variables now became the basis for forming four experimental groups out of the Ss who participated in Experiment I: (1) good retainers who are importers; (2) good retainers who are nonimporters; (3) poor retainers who are importers; (4) poor retainers who are nonimporters.

Two goals underlay this experiment. The first was to replicate the foregoing experiments, and to show that (1) the explicated versions of each story will be retained better than the original versions; (2) the good retainers will preserve the story better than the poor retainers; and (3) the importers will import more than the nonimporters.

The second goal was to explore the relationships between these variables, particularly between explication and importation. It was evident, especially in the qualitative study of the reproductions in the Exploratory Experiment, that certain importations were similar to explications, in that they were attempts to close gaps and reduce ambiguities. This function of importations—which, incidentally, also appeared conspicuously in Ss' reproductions of the theme list in Experiment I—was interpreted as revealing one of the functions of recruitment in schema formation and operation. The effects of both explication and importation seemed to converge in this recruitment process, the first providing organizing (i.e., recruitable) material in the stimulus, the second reflecting its presence in the individual as a cognitive style. Experiment II, along with the next one, offered an opportunity to study these two influences in conjunction, and to discover whether and how they interact—e.g., will they be additive or substitutive?

One expectation, based both on the findings of the foregoing experiments and on theoretical considerations, was that the importers will do better than the nonimporters on the original versions but not on the explicated versions. In the original versions importations may serve a valuable function (i.e., the same function that the experimental explications serve), while in the explicated versions they are likely to be superfluous because the text is already structured.

The present experiment was designed to yield answers to the following three empirical questions: (1) Will the importers import more in their reproductions of the original versions than in their reproductions of the explicated versions? (2) Will even the nonimporters show some importation in their reproductions of the original versions? (3) Will these differences in importation, if present, affect the accuracy and completeness with which the stories emerge from serial reproduction?

Methods and Procedures

A factorial design was planned in which each of the three main variables was to be symmetrically balanced off against the others. Therefore not one but two stimulus stories were required, each of them in both an original and explicated version. In order to achieve a fully symmetrical design, each of the four groups of Ss needed to be divided into two equivalent chains: one chain to receive the original version of story A and the explicated version of story *B*, the other to receive the explicated version of story *A* and the original version of story *B*. In this way each of the four major experimental groups (good retainers, importers; good retainers, nonimporters; poor retainers, importers; poor retainers, nonimporters) dealt with both of the stimulus stories in both versions, and comparisons were then possible between each of the main variables taken singly and in combination.

STEP 1. SELECTING GOOD AND POOR RETAINERS

Six measures (derived from Experiment I) were used as indices of retention ability: (1) the theme score of the first Bedbug reproduction (Bedbug I); (2) the number of themes lost in the course of the three Bedbug reproductions (Σ Bedbug loss); (3) the percentage of themes (based on the original composition) lost in the course of the three composition reproductions (Σ composition loss); (4) the theme-list score of the first theme-list reproduction (theme list I); (5) the total theme-list score for all three reproductions (Σ theme-list score); (6) the score on the Bedbug questionnaire.

A separate distribution for each of the six measures was prepared. It was then divided into five parts, each containing approximately the same number of *S*s, so that each of Experiment I's forty-five *S*s could be assigned a quintile score on each of the measures. A score of 5 on, say, Bedbug I meant that *S* fell in the top quintile on that measure. Obviously, anyone who had 5's on each of the six measures was one of the good retainers; one having 1's was among the poor retainers. Each *S*'s six quintile scores furnished a composite index of his retention ability.

Fortunately, because of the substantial positive correlations between the six accuracy measures, it proved relatively easy to isolate a group of *S*s who consistently fell in the top quintiles on all of the measures and a group that consistently fell in the bottom ones. Since the present experiment called for the reproduction of a story after a fifteen-minute interval, and this task is similar to the Bedbug I task, the two Bedbug measures were given the most weight among the selection criteria.

These are the criteria that I used to segregate the *S*s with respect to retention ability: (1) *Good retainers:* on the two Bedbug measures the individual must have received quintile scores of 4 or 5; on the other four measures, not more than one should have been less than 3. (2) *Poor retainers:* on the two Bedbug measures the individual must have received quintile scores of 1 or 2; on the other four measures, not more than one should have exceeded 3.

By these criteria fourteen Ss qualified as good retainers and seventeen Ss qualified as poor retainers. The remaining fourteen Ss fell toward one or the other of these poles; however, they could not meet either of the above criteria.

STEP 2. SELECTING IMPORTERS AND NONIMPORTERS

Three measures were used as indices of importation tendency: (1) the total importation score on the three theme-list reproductions (theme-list-importation score); (2) the number of themes imported in the three Bedbug reproductions (Σ Bedbug importations); (3) the number of themes imported in the three composition reproductions (Σ composition importations).

The same procedure used for assessing retention ability was used for separating the Ss into importers and nonimporters. Separate distributions were prepared for each of the three measures and each distribution was divided into five parts. Again, the substantial positive correlations between the three measures made it possible to isolate two groups: one in which no S received lower than a quintile score of 3 on any of the measures; the other in which he never exceeded 3. Nineteen Ss qualified as importers, and fourteen as nonimporters.

STEP 3. FORMING THE EXPERIMENTAL GROUPS

The procedure for forming the four experimental groups was complicated by the fact that, among the fourteen Ss who qualified as good retainers, six were importers, six were nonimporters, and two could not be classified as either; among the seventeen who qualified as poor retainers, nine were importers, only six were nonimporters, and two were unclassified. Therefore, according to the criteria for inclusion in one of the four experimental groups, only twenty-seven Ss qualified.

The experimental design, however, called for eight separate chains of Ss, two each in the four experimental groups. I had originally hoped that each chain would consist of five Ss because the Exploratory Experiment showed that such a series collapses a story adequately. The selection results just reported, however, did not provide ten qualified Ss for each of the four major groups: a strict adherence to the criteria would have provided only six Ss for three of the groups and nine for the fourth.

As a compromise, I selected six Ss among those who did not qualify on the strict basis of the criteria. They were selected on the basis of next best qualification; each fell just short of meeting the criteria. This made it possible to form the four groups with eight Ss in each, and each of the eight serial reproduction chains having four Ss.

The next task was to divide each group of eight Ss into two equivalent groups of four and to schedule them. In order to maximize the preservation of the stories through each chain, the Ss in each were ordered with respect to their retention ability: the Ss with the highest accuracy scores were put at the heads of the chains.

Most of the conclusions drawn from the present experiment must depend on the relative success of the selection and grouping of the Ss. Consequently, I made a careful assessment of this part of the procedure, some analyses done before the gathering of the serial reproduction data, some afterwards. Though my main purpose was to check the selection, some subsidiary findings emerged that are of interest in their own right.

Table 6 presents selection data on all members of the eight serial reproduction chains. The I.Q. scores are included, and show that on the average the good retainers had higher I.Q.'s than the poor retainers. This finding suggests that retention ability is related to a more general intellectual ability. On the other hand, I.Q. was not related to importation tendency: the importers achieved a mean I.Q. of 112.2, the nonimporters 112.7.

Table 6, containing the selection data from Experiment I, can reveal whether there were any unwanted differences between the four groups. For example, was there a systematic difference in accuracy scores between the two good retainer groups (were the importers, say, better than the nonimporters)? No differences of this kind appear. In only one respect was there a difference between the groups: among the importers, the poor retainers did significantly more importing than did the good retainers (among the nonimporters a small trend in this direction is also evident). This difference, therefore, will have to be taken into account in later analyses of the data. Fortunately, this relationship in itself was not of central interest, unlike the relationship between importing and explication. Since each group dealt with both versions of each story, the relationship between importation and explication was not contaminated by retention ability.

Table 6
SELECTION DATA ON THE EXPERIMENTAL GROUPS

Group	Order	I.Q.	Retention Ability						Importation		
			Bedbug I Theme Score	Total Bedbug Theme Loss	Total Composition Theme Loss'	Theme List I Score	Total Theme List Score	Questionnaire Score	Total Bedbug Theme Importations	Total Composition Theme Importations	Total Theme List Importation Score
Good Retainers, Importers	No. 1	120	23	5	5%	30	88	20	9	1	17
	No. 2	105	21	3	7%	27	80	20	7	2	14
	No. 3	143	24	2	18%	25	66	18	5	5	13
	No. 4	100	21	9	12%	30	88	19	5	2	15
	Mean of Chain	117.0	22.3	4.8	8.8%	28.0	80.5	19.3	6.5	2.5	14.8
	No. 1	123	23	3	9%	32	77	20	4	4	16
	No. 2	104	22	3	10%	31	80	18	8	4	13
	No. 3	115	23	2	20%	19	51	21	12	10	14
	No. 4	123	22	8	22%	37	102	20.5	9	4	15
	Mean of Chain	116.3	22.5	4.0	15.3%	29.8	77.5	19.9	8.3	5.5	14.5
Good Retainers	No. 1	120	22	0	9%	33	89	21	1	2	8
	No. 2	115	23	3	5%	35	101	21	6	2	8
	No. 3	114	22	4	4%	19	35	22	3	5	6
	No. 4	123	20	10	5%	33	93	22	6	1	6
	Mean of Chain	118.0	21.8	4.3	5.8%	30.0	79.5	21.5	4.0	2.5	7.0

Table 6 (Continued)

Nonimporters	No. 1	116	22	1	3%	35	88	21	2	5	6
	No. 2	112	19	5	23%	29	82	21	4	5	9
	No. 3	123	22	5	16%	37	105	19	1	5	6
	No. 4	112	22	7	9%	30	76	21	3	3	12
	Mean of Chain	115.8	21.3	4.5	12.8%	32.8	87.8	20.5	2.5	4.5	8.3
Poor Retainers, Importers	No. 1	107	21	10	21%	23	70	17	10	7	26
	No. 2	102	30	11	17%	10	37	16	10	4	19
	No. 3	119	20	14	16%	18	34	20	15	5	16
	No. 4	111	14	32	19%	20	48	15.5	12	2	24
	Mean of Chain	109.8	18.8	16.8	18.3%	17.8	47.5	17.1	11.8	4.5	21.3
	No. 1	102	20	10	39%	25	62	19.5	17	9	25
	No. 2	105	18	19	40%	19	46	17	9	5	24
	No. 3	106	21	16	43%	37	74	15	7	9	18
	No. 4	110	16	22	19%	17	40	11.5	19	7	18
	Mean of Chain	105.8	18.8	16.8	35.3%	24.5	55.5	15.8	13.0	7.5	21.3
Poor Retainers, Nonimporters	No. 1	123	23	14	20%	32	78	18.5	3	3	10
	No. 2	113	19	11	30%	27	74	18	5	2	12
	No. 3	115	16	35	23%	32	84	14.5	1	1	12
	No. 4	102	18	28	51%	13	20	11	7	3	10
	Mean of Chain	113.3	19.0	22.0	31.0%	26.0	64.0	15.5	4.0	2.3	11.0
	No. 1	124	22	9	32%	28	69	16	2	2	5
	No. 2	93	20	8	5%	25	69	17	9	3	8
	No. 3	96	21	17	30%	20	45	17.5	6	4	8
	No. 4	102	20	24	40%	25	33	16	3	4	8
	Mean of Chain	103.8	20.8	14.5	26.8%	24.5	54.0	16.6	5.0	3.3	7.3

Some further checks of the selection data were made to see what differences existed among the eight groups, particularly on those tasks that most resemble the serial reproduction task. The relevant tasks in Experiment I were Bedbug I and theme list I, since they each involved the reproduction of a text fifteen minutes after two perusals (which is exactly what each member of the serial chains does in the present experiment). In addition to a theme analysis, I also made an information-unit analysis of the Bedbug I reproductions. These results, and the result of an information-unit analysis of the theme-list I reproductions, are presented in Table 7.[9]

With respect to retention ability and explication, the results are unequivocal: in all three measures the good retainer chains were clearly superior to the poor retainer chains; and each of the four experimental groups was successfully divided, so that the chain which received the original version of the Ghost Story was not significantly different from its counterpart which received the explicated version. Moreover, a measure of success was achieved in the scheduling procedure: at least the first members of each chain were the best retainers, even though the second and third positions were reversed.

However, with respect to importation the results are somewhat ambiguous, even though only one of the three measures (the information-unit analysis) achieved any degree of statistical significance. Nevertheless, since the nonimporters were somewhat superior to the importers in five of the six comparisons (the theme analysis in the case of the good retainers is the sole exception), one must conclude that, in this experimental sample, the nonimporters started with an edge in retention ability over the importers.[10]

I also made a further check on importations in these selection

---

[9] Since each chain received only one version of both stories (the original version of one, the explicated version of the other), Table 7 locates the chains only with respect to the Ghost Story (with respect to the second story the table is simply duplicated). The Ss were scheduled in the order of their retention ability, and, since it is necessary to know how successfully this ordering was done, Table 7 presents the mean for each position in the chains in addition to the mean of the chains.

[10] Whereas the nonimporters were superiors to the importers, this difference was greater among the good retainers than among the poor ones, while, in the subsequent serial reproductions, the reverse was true (see below, pp. 90-92). It is difficult to know whether this edge was big enough to account for the subsequent superiority of the nonimporters in many of the serial reproduction measures. However, it should be noted that the serial repoduction technique usually enhances and exaggerates retention processes and thus a small edge may prove efficacious.

Table 7

EXPERIMENTAL GROUPS' MEAN ACCURACY SCORES ON BEDBUG I AND THEME LIST I

		Theme Score	Information Score	Theme List Score
Ghost Story	Original Group	20.5	62.2	25.5
	Explicated Group	20.8	61.4	27.8
Good Retainers	Importers	22.4	63.8	28.9
	Nonimporters	21.5	74.9	31.4
Poor Retainers	Importers	18.8	51.6	21.1
	Nonimporters	19.9	56.9	25.3
Serial Order	Position No. 1	22.0	66.3	29.6
	Position No. 2	20.3	55.6	25.4
	Position No. 3	21.1	66.1	25.9
	Position No. 4	19.1	59.1	25.6

ANALYSIS OF VARIANCE

Source	D.F.	F-Ratio			P		
		Theme Score	Information Score	Theme List Score	Theme Score	Information Score	Theme List Score
Explication	1:25	—	—	1.21	—	—	—
Retention Ability	1:25	19.51	20.70	9.78	.001	.001	.01
Importation	1:25	—	6.11	2.23	—	.05	—
Serial Order	3:25	4.28	2.54	—	.05	.05	—

data by scoring each S's Bedbug I reproduction for importations at the information-unit level to see what differences existed between the Ss who formed the eight experimental chains. Table 8, which presents this analysis, shows that only one difference between the main groups is significant: it is the built-in difference—the importers imported more than did the nonimporters. The groups which later received the original version of the Ghost Story (the O-groups)—who did more importing in it than did those who got the explicated version—showed a slightly smaller tendency to import on Bedbug I than did the latter. However, this initial difference between the O- and E-groups is not of significant proportions.

Table 8

EXPERIMENTAL GROUPS' MEAN

IMPORTATION SCORES ON BEDBUG I

Ghost Story	Original Group	8.1
	Explicated Group	10.8
	Total	9.5
Importers	Good Retainers	15.5
	Poor Retainers	13.8
	Total	14.7
Nonimporters	Good Retainers	4.0
	Poor Retainers	4.6
	Total	4.3

ANALYSIS OF VARIANCE

Source	D.F.	F-Ratio	P
Explication	1:25	1.76	—
Retention Ability	1:25	—	—
Importation	1:25	25.86	> .001
Serial Order	3:25	—	—

RETENTION STYLE AND RETENTION ABILITY

One may conclude that, in all respects but one, the eight experimental groups differed from each other only in those respects upon which they were segregated. The only unwanted difference existed between the importers and nonimporters in retention ability. The difference was neither substantial nor consistent enough to attain statistical significance; nevertheless, since the serial reproduction method magnifies trends, it may prove efficacious in the present experiment. Therefore the superiority of the nonimporters must be borne in mind in assessing the results of the present experiment.

STEP 4. A SECOND STIMULUS STORY: THE POTLATCH STORY

The design of the present experiment called for a second story, in both an original and explicated form, to be used in conjunction with the Ghost Story. I selected another Indian folk story, called "The Origin of the Potlatch," which is roughly equivalent in size and character to the Ghost Story. It has the foreign ring, the gaps and ambiguities. It has 326 words (compared to the Ghost's 333), twenty themes (compared to the Ghost's 23), 128 information units (compared to the Ghost's 130), and a redundancy index of 6.40. This is the original version of the story.

The Potlatch Story: Original Version

The Origin / of the Potlatch /

a) A strange / bird / once appeared / in the ocean / in front / of the village. / *b*) All the young men / of the Quillayute / went out and tried / to shoot it, / but no one could hit it. / *c*) Every day / Blue Jay, / a slave / of Golden Eagle, / watched / the hunters / try to shoot / the strange bird. /

d) One day / Golden Eagle / said to / Blue Jay, / "Eh, my children / can catch / that queer-looking bird." /

e) "Oh, no," / replied / Blue Jay. / "They are girls." /

f) Golden Eagle's / daughters / overheard the two. / *g*) Next day / the two / younger / sisters / went into the woods / and stayed / all day. / Many days / they spent / in the woods, / telling no one / what they were doing. / *h*) Although they were girls, / just imagine / —they were making arrows! /

i) One morning, / before daylight, / they went to the forest / and brought in / the arrows they had made. / When they returned / to the village, / all the hunters / had gone out / in their canoes /

to try again / to shoot / the strange-looking bird. / *j*) The two sisters / tied / their hair / in front. / No one / could recognize them. / *k*) Then they paddled / their canoe / in a zigzag line / until they were near the bird. / *l*) The older / of the sisters / killed it / with her third / arrow. /

m) That evening / the girls / said to their father, / "We caught / the bird / and then we hid it / in the woods. / *n*) We want to use / its feathers / as presents, / for the feathers / are of many colors. / *o*) Will you tell / Blue Jay / to invite / all the birds / to come to our lodge / tomorrow?" /

p) Next morning / all kinds / of birds / were gathered / in the lodge / of Golden Eagle. / *q*) "My daughters / caught / the strange bird," / the host / explained, / "they want to give / each of you / a present." / *r*) The girls / gave / certain colors / to different birds. / They gave / to each bird / the colors / it was to have. /

s) Ever since then, / certain birds / have had / certain colors. / And since then, / there have been potlatches. / *t*) This was the first / potlatch, / the first giving / of gifts / from the people who invite / to the people who are invited. /

STEP 5. THE POTLATCH STORY EXPLICATED

I prepared an explicated version of this story, following roughly the procedure used for the Ghost Story explication. However, in the Potlatch Story, I attempted a more thoroughgoing yet piecemeal explication. I made many changes in wording to remove ambiguities, inserted many new clarifying and simplifying clauses, and changed the word order at several places. On the other hand, I added only one wholly new theme [to replace theme *o*)]. In order to equalize the two versions for word count, I omitted a number of parts of the Potlatch Story which seemed to be superfluous [primarily in themes *c*) and *i*)].

This version has a redundancy index of 6.30, which is slightly lower than that of the original version (6.40), and reveals that the extensive piecemeal explication and the omissions had the effect of reducing the redundancy of the story.[11] This is the explicated version of the Potlatch Story; the changed as well as new parts are italicized.

---

[11] Some possible consequences of this are discussed below on p. 98.

The Potlatch Story: Explicated Version

The Origin / of the Potlatch /

a) A strange / bird / appeared once / *over* the ocean / near / the bird-village / where all the birds / of the earth / lived / once upon a time. / *b*) All the young *hunters* / of the Quillayute, / *the bird-people*, / went out and tried / to shoot it, / but no one could hit it. / *c*) Every day / Blue Jay / watched / the hunters / try to shoot / the strange bird. /

d) One day / Golden Eagle / said to / Blue Jay, / "Eh, my children / can catch / that queer-looking bird." /

e) "Oh, no, / they are girls," / replied / Blue Jay. /

f) Golden Eagle's / daughters / *were nearby* / and overheard / *the conversation*. / *g*) Next day / the two / young*est of them* / went into the woods / and stayed *there* / all day. / Many days / they spent / in the woods, / telling no one / what they were doing. / *h*) They were making arrows—*but they were special / ones*! /

i) One morning, / before daylight, / they went to the forest / *to bring home* / the *special* arrows. / *j*) When they returned / to the village, / the two sisters / tied / their hair / in front / *to disguise themselves*. / *k*) Then they paddled / their canoe / in a zigzag line / *so the bird wouldn't* / *notice* / *that they were approaching*. / *l*) The older / of the sisters / killed it / with her third / arrow. /

m) That evening / the girls / said to their father, / "We caught / the bird / and then we hid it / in the woods. / Its feathers / are of many colors. / *n*) Since we all in the village / have only / grey / feathers, / let us all take / of these feathers / and we shall be beautiful. / *o*) This will be a real / present / to everybody / and our people / will know / that giving presents / is a great virtue." /

p) Next morning / all the birds / were gathered / in the lodge / of Golden Eagle. / *q*) "My daughters / caught / the strange bird," / the host / explained. / "They want to give / each of you / a present." / *r*) The girls / gave / to *each* bird / different-*colored* / feathers. / They gave / to each bird / the colors / it was to have. /

s) Ever since then, / certain birds / have had / certain colors. / And since then, / there have been potlatches. / *t*) *which are ceremonies* / *in which the host* / *gives presents* / *to his guests*. / This was the first / potlatch. /

STEP 6. CONDUCT OF THE EXPERIMENT

The serial reproductions were obtained by the same procedure used in the Exploratory Experiment. The *S*s participated in groups of ten: one member from each of the eight chains plus a member from each of the "residue" chains of importers and skeletonizers. I administered both stories—the Ghost Story always preceding the Potlatch Story—in one sixty-minute session. A concentration task requiring S to strike out the vowels in a typewritten text was interpolated between each learning and reproduction.

The boys continued to be cooperative. In view of the fact that the task was quite arduous, and that each had already spent three hours performing similar tasks, it seemed remarkable that there was only an occasional expression of exasperation and weariness.

Results

The measures used in the Exploratory Experiment and Experiment I were applied to the serial reproductions of Experiment II. The differences between stories and between groups were statistically assessed by the analysis of variance technique,[12] separate analyses for each of the main measures.

1. ACCURACY ANALYSES

The first analysis is of the total theme score of each chain[13] and is presented in Table 9 along with the results of the analysis of variance. It shows that three of the variables made significant differences: the explicated versions of both stories were reproduced more accurately than the original versions; the good retainers did better than the poor retainers; and the Potlatch Story was reproduced better than the Ghost Story. When the results of good and poor retainers were combined, there was no difference between the importers and nonimporters; when they were separated, however, a significant difference did emerge:[14] among the good retainers, the

---

[12] This technique reveals the level of significance of differences between means derived from a balanced design. It is described and discussed in most standard textbooks on statistics (see, for example, McNemar, 1949).

[13] The raw data upon which this and the subsequent analyses are based are too cumbersome for presentation here. Moreover, for purposes of the present analyses it was often necessary to transform each raw score to a percentage based on the stimulus stories since they contain different numbers of themes and information units.

[14] The double-interaction Retention Ability X Importation represents this finding. Only those few higher-order interactions that proved significant are included in the tables. It should be noted that the comparatively small number of cases in each cell along with the fact that each independent variable is represented by only two values (hence has only one degree-of-freedom) made it difficult for any higher-order interaction to attain significance.

Table 9

MEAN THEME SCORES OF THE CHAINS, COMPUTED AS PERCENTAGES
BASED ON THE ORIGINAL STIMULUS STORIES

Groups		Stories						Total
		Original Version			Explicated Version			
		Ghost	Potlatch	Total	Ghost	Potlatch	Total	
Good Retainers	Importers	54.3	73.8	64.1	67.7	71.3	69.5	66.8
	Nonimporters	61.9	58.8	60.4	70.8	71.3	71.1	65.7
	Total	58.1	66.3	62.2	69.3	71.3	70.3	66.2
Poor Retainers	Importers	41.3	56.3	48.8	47.9	56.3	52.1	50.5
	Nonimporters	51.1	66.3	58.7	63.5	67.5	65.5	62.1
	Total	46.2	61.3	53.8	55.7	61.9	58.8	56.3
Total		52.2	63.8	58.0	62.5	66.6	64.6	

ANALYSIS OF VARIANCE

Source	D.F.	F-Ratio	P
Explication	1:10	6.81	< .05
Retention Ability	1:11	10.52	< .01
Importation	1:11	2.96	—
Stories	1:10	9.84	< .05
Retention Ability X Importation	1:5	9.90	< .05

importers did slightly, though not significantly, better than the nonimporters; among the poor ones, the nonimporters did considerably and significantly better than the importers.

The relationship between explication and importation, though it falls short of statistical significance, is worth inspecting because of its theoretical importance. Table 9 shows that, among the good retainers, the importers did better than the nonimporters on the original versions of the stories, while on the explicated versions the reverse was true. Among the poor retainers, the nonimporters exceeded the importers on both versions but they did so to a greater extent on the explicated versions (they were 9.9 per cent better on the original, and 13.4 per cent better on the explicated). Combining both groups, explication seems to have made almost twice as much difference to the nonimporters as it did to the importers (17.5 per cent to 8.9 per cent).

The analysis of the more molecular information scores,[15] presented in Table 10, follows the theme analysis quite closely. All of the main variables exerted significant effects: both explicated versions were reproduced more accurately than the original versions; the good retainers were superior to the poor ones; the nonimporters of both groups did better than the importers; and the Potlatch Story fared better than the Ghost Story. In this analysis, as in the first, the positive effect of explication was greater on the nonimporters than on the importers. This was true primarily of the good retainers: for the importers, explication made an average difference of 7.9 units; for the nonimporters it resulted in a 10.9 average improvement. Among the poor retainers the relationship is much smaller: it made a 6.1 unit difference for the importers and a 6.8 difference for the nonimporters.

To sum up: The two main accuracy measures yielded results that are in line with expectation and corroborate the effects of explication and retention ability. The nonimporters did somewhat better than the importers in accuracy of reproduction, and the Potlatch Story was superior to the Ghost Story. Finally, explication had a different influence upon importers and nonimporters. The fact that explication made less difference to the importers is in line with

---

[15] This analysis dealt with the raw scores. A separate analysis was also made on the percentages, with identical results.

Table 10

MEAN INFORMATION SCORES OF THE CHAINS

Groups		Original Version			Explicated Version			Total
		Ghost	Potlatch	Total	Ghost	Potlatch	Total	
Good Retainers	Importers	38.25	48.75	43.50	48.75	54.00	51.38	47.44
	Nonimporters	45.25	46.25	45.75	52.50	60.50	56.50	51.13
	Total	41.75	47.50	44.63	50.63	57.25	53.94	49.29
Poor Retainers	Importers	26.25	35.00	30.63	36.00	40.25	38.13	34.38
	Nonimporters	32.50	43.25	37.88	42.00	46.00	44.00	40.94
	Total	29.38	39.13	34.26	39.00	43.13	41.07	37.67
Total		35.57	43.32	39.45	44.82	50.19	47.51	

ANALYSIS OF VARIANCE

Source	D.F.	F-Ratio	P
Explication	1:11	46.32	> .001
Retention Ability	1:11	96.29	> .001
Importation	1:11	18.72	> .01
Stories	1:11	30.69	> .001

the expectation based on the overlapping functions of these two variables.

In addition to these two main accuracy analyses, I made a number of others that merit presentation here. Separate examination of the lead-off reproductions of each chain is important, because each of them had the experimental stimulus story as its stimulus rather than a second- or third-hand version of it. Table 11 presents both the theme and information unit analyses of the eight No. 1 reproductions. In both measures the good retainers were superior to the poor ones, and the nonimporters did better than the importers. Both explicated versions were reproduced more accurately than were the original versions. In the theme analysis, however, this was true only for the Ghost Story. The Potlatch Story was reproduced better than the Ghost Story, particularly in the information-unit analysis.

Further analysis of the lead-off reproduction failed to corroborate the finding, which the analysis of the total chains pointed up, that explication had a greater effect on the nonimporters. Nevertheless, Table 11 shows that there was a small difference in line with this relationship, and it may be that this small initial difference was progressively magnified by the subsequent serial reproductions. The difference had become pronounced in the final reproductions of each chain, which I also analyzed separately.

Analysis of the final reproductions yielded virtually identical results, except that the nonimporters were only slightly (and not significantly) superior to the importers, and the relationship between explication and importation, which was slight in the lead-off reproductions and quite noticeable in the chains as a whole, is now substantial. A comparison of the theme scores of the final reproductions showed that the importers reproduced the explicated versions on the whole neither better nor worse than the original versions, while the explicated versions of the nonimporters were superior to the original versions by eleven themes. Similarly, in information score, the nonimporters exceeded the importers by an average of four units in the amount they favored the explicated versions.

Following the procedure I used in the Exploratory Experiment, I rescored each reproduction against the standard of its own stimulus text (the previous serial reproduction). Since this kind

Table 11

MEAN ACCURACY SCORES OF THE NO. 1 REPRODUCTIONS, COMPUTED AS PERCENTAGES BASED ON THE STIMULUS STORIES

		Theme Score	Information Score
Ghost Story	Original Version	77.0	46.7
	Explicated Version	93.8	60.2
	Total	85.4	53.6
Potlatch Story	Original Version	88.8	61.4
	Explicated Version	88.8	65.7
	Total	88.8	63.5
Good Retainers	Importers	87.5	56.0
	Nonimporters	97.5	68.9
	Total	92.5	62.5
Poor Retainers	Importers	77.0	51.5
	Nonimporters	86.2	57.6
	Total	81.6	54.5

ANALYSIS OF VARIANCE

Source	D.F.	F-Ratio Themes	F-Ratio Information	P Theme	P Information
Explication	1:11	—	7.89	—	> .05
Retention Ability	1:11	15.51	6.29	> .01	> .05
Importation	1:11	12.15	8.99	> .01	> .05
Stories	1:11	1.49	10.11	—	> .01
Stories X Explication	1:5	7.16	—	> .05	—

of analysis appraises each reproduction on its own merits and does not compound errors (i.e., if No. 1 committed an error, and if the rest of the chain accurately reproduced this error, this single error was quadrupled in the final score), it can be expected to show whether the experimental variables exerted their influence throughout the chains. I made two separate analyses of these data, the first including all Ss, the second excluding the lead-off member of each chain. The results of both these analyses proved wholly corroborative and, since they are largely identical to those already reported, I will not repeat them in detail. They revealed that the three main variables continued to exert significant effects in the expected direction, and that the effect of explication was greatest on the nonimporters.

Word-count analyses of the serial reproductions are of minor interest. The only statistically significant finding was that the good retainers' reproductions were longer than those of the poor retainers. Among the former, the importers' reproductions were longer than the nonimporters'; among the latter, this was reversed. For all groups the explicated versions exceeded the original versions, but this finding failed to attain statistical significance.

2. IMPORTATION ANALYSIS

Did the importers do more importing than the nonimporters? Did all Ss import more in their reproductions of the original versions of the stories than of the explicated versions? These were the main questions for an importation analysis of the serial reproductions.

The analysis was done as follows. Every information unit and theme that appeared in a reproduction and was not present even in the form of a synonym in the original stimulus story was counted as an importation. Each of these importations was then judged as "major" or "minor," on the basis of its degree of departure from the original text.[16] Since the judgment of major and minor is largely a subjective one, the following analyses were done both on this importation score (which is computed by scoring each major importation 2 points and each minor importation 1 point) and on the number of importations, disregarding the major-minor assessment.

Table 12 presents the mean importation score and the mean number of importations in each of the serial reproductions, and the results of an analysis of variance. Only one of the main variables

---

[16] A more complete description of this procedure is presented on p. 69. The present scoring was carried out by a trained assistant who worked without access to any information that might indicate from which group any reproduction came and hence prejudice the scoring.

Table 12

MEAN NUMBER OF IMPORTATIONS AND MEAN IMPORTATION SCORE OF EACH REPRODUCTION

		Ghost Story				Potlatch Story				Total	
		Original Version		Explicated Version		Original Version		Explicated Version			
		No.	Score	No.	Score	No.	Score	No.	Score	No.	Score
Importers	Good Retainers	4.8	7.5	4.0	6.3	4.3	6.5	5.0	8.3	4.5	7.1
	Poor Retainers	4.0	6.3	3.0	4.5	3.0	4.8	4.0	6.8	3.5	5.6
	Total	4.4	6.9	3.5	5.4	3.7	5.7	4.5	7.6	4.0	6.4
Nonimporters	Good Retainers	2.0	2.8	1.0	1.3	1.5	2.3	2.0	3.5	1.6	2.5
	Poor Retainers	3.3	5.0	2.5	3.5	3.8	4.8	3.5	5.3	3.5	4.6
	Total	2.7	3.9	1.8	2.4	2.7	3.6	2.8	4.4	2.6	3.6
Total		3.6	5.4	2.7	3.9	3.2	4.7	3.7	6.0		

ANALYSIS OF VARIANCE*

Source	D.F.	F-Ratio	P
Importation	1:11	15.01	>.01
Stories	1:11	—	—
Explication	1:11	—	—
Retention Ability	1:11	—	—
Story X Explication	1:5	93.10	>.001
Importation X Retention	1:5	158.38	>.001

* Based on the Importation Score Data.

exerts a significant effect, the expected one: the importers did more importing than the nonimporters.

Two interesting results emerge in the form of interactions between the variables. First, while the original version of the Ghost Story was subjected to more importation than was the explicated version on the part of importers *and nonimporters,* this was completely reversed in the case of the Potlatch Story—here the explicated version underwent more importation than did the original version. Second, among the importers, the good retainers did more importing (on both stories, in both versions) than the poor retainers; among the nonimporters, it is the poor retainers who did more importing. (Though it failed to attain statistical significance there, this finding was also present in the selection data; see Table 8.)

Summary and Conclusions

The Exploratory Experiment revealed a congruent relationship between explication and importation that could be understood in terms of their convergence on the process of recruitment. Therefore, one of the expectations underlying the present expriment was that more importing would occur on the original versions of the stories than on the explicated versions. This expectation was confirmed, but only in the case of the Ghost Story. On the Potlatch Story it was the explicated version that underwent more importation. Why should the explication in one case favor importation, and in the other case not?

The answer may lie in the fact that my explication of these two stories differed in some important respects, as already described. Of these, the different effect of explication of the redundancy indexes may be of particular importance. It may be that redundancy is a major determinant of the degree to which a text tends to undergo importation during serial reproduction. This possibility is worth further exploration, since it points to an important function that importation may be serving: namely, the enhancement of redundancy—a possibility that was already suggested in the Exploratory Experiment. The following experiment, Experiment III, offered a good opportunity to examine this relationship in detail.

The importation variable itself stood up very well in the present experiment: the chains of importers showed more importation than those of the nonimporters. The accuracy results were also in line with expectations: the explicated versions of both the Ghost and Potlatch Stories[17] were more accurately reproduced than the original versions; and the good retainers consistently showed their superiority over the poor retainers. This held true for the chains as a whole, for the chains minus the lead-off reproduction, separately for the lead-off and final reproductions, and whether accuracy was scored on the basis of the original stimulus stories or on each reproduction's own stimulus text. All in all, the results of Experiment II provide further support for the efficacy of the stimulus variable explication, and speak strongly for the stability and relative generality of both retention ability and importation style.

Two important relationships between variables emerged: between retention ability and importation, and between explication and importation. The first, contrary to the impressions gained from the Exploratory Experiment and also to the results of Experiment I, suggests that the ability and style variables are not wholly independent from each other, but that there is a small negative relationship between them. The fact that, particularly among the poor retainers in the present experiment, the nonimporters did better than the importers can probably be traced to the small but consistent difference between the groups (revealed by careful analysis of the relevant selection data) which the serial transmission method magnified. This relationship is further explored in Experiment III.

The second relationship has noteworthy theoretical implications. Explication had a greater effect upon the nonimporters than upon the importers. This was especially true among the good retainers and became particularly apparent at the ends of the chains, though to some extent this relationship also occurred among the poor retainers and was also detectable in the lead-off reproductions.

This finding may be viewed as another testimony to the congruence or overlapping functions of explication and importation. The importer does not benefit as much from text explications be-

[17] The fact that the Potlatch Story was reproduced better than the Ghost Story is only of minor interest, and is probably due to the various properties of the stories in addition to the possibility that its contents were more familiar to the Ss. Since the order of administration of the two stories was not alternated (the Potlatch came second), it is not possible to rule out position and fatigue effects.

cause he himself, in importing, furnishes such explications. His schemas normally build up and function with a heavier emphasis on recruitment, so that the explications that are provided in the story in order to serve this function are superfluous or redundant. To the nonimporter, however, these organizing and integrating parts of the story are far from superfluous because of the absence in him of reliance on recruitment. In a way, the explicated version of the story contains within it materials for recruitment which compensate for the relative absence of it in the nonimporter's schema formation. Both explication and importation serve to enhance redundancy and assure the coherence and continuity of schema structure.

But before discussing these theoretical implications further let us go on with the final experiment in this series, which continues to explore and examine the relationship among the variables, and also includes the familiarity variable.

EXPERIMENT III: IMPORTING IN RELATION TO EXPLICATION AND FAMILIARITY

Purpose

The present experiment, which introduced importation style into the design of the Exploratory Experiment, was designed mainly to study the relationship of importation to familiarity, and to re-examine the relationship between importation and explication. Essentially, this experiment was a final replication and integration of the foregoing studies, which can be summed up briefly in the following way:

The Exploratory Experiment demonstrated the efficacy of two stimulus variables, explication and familiarity; it also brought into relief the phenomenon of importing, which occurred particularly in the reproductions of the less familiar and unexplicated stories. Experiments I and II isolated two subject variables, importation style and retention ability, and also revealed that explications had a greater effect on nonimporters than on importers. This finding, together with the results of a detailed examination of the reproductions of the Exploratory Experiment, suggested that importation and explication play overlapping or congruent roles in the formation and functioning of schemas—both converging on the schema process of recruitment. Familiarity of text and importation are also related, in a reciprocal way; there was less importing on the more familiar story. I therefore proposed that familiarity with the content of a stimulus, by assuring the presence of appropriate schemas, should, like explication, facilitate schema formation.

All of the findings made clear that importation, explication, and familiarity are closely related and that each contributes to the coherence and continuity of schemas underlying learning and retention. Experiment III was a final test of this general proposition and another attempt to explore the relationship among the variables.

Methods and Procedures

The design of Experiment III, since it was borrowed from the foregoing studies, can be stated briefly. In order to assure and enhance the familiarity of the Secretary Story (which was designed in the first place for Ss who were secretaries), secretarial students at the end of their final year of training were chosen to serve as Ss. The experiment was divided into two parts. The first part corresponded to Experiment I, and consisted of a procedure to test a population of Ss for retention ability and importation style. The second part corresponded to Experiment II, and consisted of a serial reproduction procedure with relatively homogeneous groups of importers and nonimporters selected from the larger population.

The design called for two groups of Ss (one of importers, the other of nonimporters), each to be divided into two subgroups of five Ss each, one subgroup of each main group to receive the original version of the Ghost Story, the other to receive the explicated version. All four groups were composed of good retainers, were equated for retention ability, and were scheduled so that the best retainers led off each chain.

MODIFIED THEME-LIST TECHNIQUE FOR ASSESSING IMPORTATION

I modified the theme-list technique somewhat for this experiment. In Experiment I the theme list was first learned by S in a free manner (he was told merely to "get to know" the list of themes); the next step was the composition based on the theme list, after which the theme list was reproduced. This procedure does not assess the original learning of the theme list, and so does not provide a way to detect what the *S* imported into the reproduction of the theme list from the composition in order to distinguish it from what he merely failed to learn in the first place. Therefore, I modified the technique to include a reproduction of the theme list *before* the composition as well as a reproduction following the composition. A comparison of these two reproductions provides for the detection of importations that are directly attributable to the composition—each of the differences between the pre- and post-theme-list reproductions can be referred directly to the composition to see whether it is reflected there or not. Only new material that is contained in the composition is scored as an importation.

This is the modified first instruction (the other instructions were unchanged):

> You have each been handed a typewritten sheet. It contains a list of themes of a story called "Balanced Rock." I would like you to read this list of themes carefully and get to know the themes of this story. Please read the list through twice, carefully but at your usual reading speed. When you are through, turn this sheet face down and look up. Are there any questions? Remember, get to know the list of themes by reading through the material carefully twice in succession. When you are finished, turn the sheet over and look up. Please go ahead now.

This method also provides an assessment of each *S*'s retention ability: the accuracy and completeness of the first reproduction of the theme list which is uncontaminated by any relevant interpolated task. The two measures necessary for forming the groups of *S*s were thus derived from a single procedure.

STEP 1. TESTING FOR IMPORTATION STYLE AND RETENTION ABILITY

Approximately one month before their graduation from a public high school, the senior class of female secretarial students—110 girls ranging in age from fifteen and a half to seventeen—was assembled for a fifty-minute period, and I administered the modified theme-list technique. Each *S* provided three pieces of data: a composition based on the theme list, and two reproductions of the theme list, one before and the other after the composition. A coding technique was used to assure anonymity.

STEP 2. SELECTING IMPORTERS AND NONIMPORTERS

The data that emerged from the selection procedure were treated in essentially the same way as in the foregoing experiments.[18] First I scored each theme-list reproduction I for accuracy and completeness at the level of information units. This score served as the main index of retention ability.

I ranked the Ss with respect to their theme list I scores and selected the twenty-four top-ranking Ss to serve as experimental Ss.[19] Next, I scored these Ss' theme-list reproductions II for importations (i.e., new information units traceable to the composition) and separated them into two equal groups: the twelve having the highest number of importations and the twelve having the lowest.

It turned out that those Ss who showed the greater importing tendency fell in the lower part of the rank ordering with respect to retention ability. Among the five best retainers, only one was an importer; among the next eight, only three were importers. Therefore it was not possible to select a group of twelve importers who were equivalent in retention ability to a group of twelve nonimporters. However, it was possible to divide up each group into two parts which were equivalent in this respect. Four groups of six Ss each were thus provided: two groups of importers matched in retention ability, and two groups of nonimporters also matched to each other but superior as a group to the importers.

In order to maximize the preservation of the stories during serial reproduction, I tried, as before, to schedule the Ss so that in each chain the best retainers came first. Even though absences, and the like, prevented this scheduling from being fulfilled completely, nevertheless, as Table 13 shows, the scheduling was fairly successful.

Table 13 shows the four groups, their selection data, and the way they were scheduled. It also shows each S's score on the Terman-McNemar Test of Mental Ability Form D, which was administered at the beginning of the semester by the school psychologist. The table includes the number of *new* importations in each S's third reproduction of the theme list, which was obtained after she had participated in the serial reproduction chain, between seven and

---

[18] The scoring techniques are described on pp. 68-70.
[19] I selected four more than the twenty called for by the experimental design, so that each of the four subgroups would have a substitute in the event of absence or defection.

Table 13

SELECTION DATA ON THE EXPERIMENTAL GROUPS

Order	Original Group				Explicated Group			
	I.Q.	Theme List I Score	No. Importations in Theme List II	No. Importations in Theme List III	I.Q.	Theme List I Score	No. Importations in Theme List II	No. Importations in Theme List III
Importers								
No. 1	110	67	5	0(2)*	119	59	2	0(1)
No. 2	121	51	3	3	125	59	3	4(3)
No. 3	110	42	2	3	107	37	7	2
No. 4	116	46	5	0	108	47	4	0(1)
No. 5	108	32	6(1)	0(2)	110	35	4(2)	2
Mean of Chain	113.0	47.6	4.2	1.2	113.8	47.4	4.0	1.6
Nonimporters								
No. 1	112	66	2	0(2)	104	67	0	3
No. 2	100	54	1	2(2)	99	61	0	—
No. 3	104	62	1	1	105	54	0	0
No. 4	105	52	2(2)	0	126	67	1	2
No. 5	92	51	1	1	89	57	0	2
Mean of Chain	102.6	57.0	1.4	0.8	104.6	61.2	0.2	1.4

*Those importations which cannot be traced to the $\underline{S}$'s composition are in parentheses.

nine days following the selection procedure. Included in parentheses are those importations that could not be located in S's composition and so were not counted in the main score.

In order to see whether the modified method of assessing importation resulted in scores significantly different from those obtained by the original method, I also scored each theme list I for importations in the original way. This analysis showed the methods to be highly congruent, since those Ss who were assigned to the importer groups on the basis of the modified method had more importations in their theme-list I reproductions than those who were assigned to the nonimporter groups (the means were 3.5 and 1.7 respectively). However, the lead-off members of the two importer chains each gave only one importation in their theme-list I reproductions, a fact that may be important in evaluating their performance on the serial reproductions. Incidentally, it is noteworthy that there are more instances of nontraceable importations in theme list III than in theme list II, indicating that a relatively long interval results in increasing recruitment of distant or unrelated material.

Table 13 shows that the nonimporters were significantly superior to the importers in their theme-list I accuracy scores. The former achieved a mean score of 59.10 and the latter 47.50.[20] The question arose: does this relationship contradict the finding of Experiments I and II that importation style was not significantly correlated with retention ability? To answer this question, I scored the theme-list reproductions of the entire population from which these twenty Ss were selected, and found that the nonimporters scored a mean of 38.57 against the importers' 35.58. The difference between these means is considerably smaller than that between the experimental groups, and it fails to achieve statistical significance ($t = 0.25$). Moreover, the correlation between number of importations and theme-list I scores based on the entire population of Ss (including those selected) proved small and without statistical significance.[21]

It is noteworthy that the nonimporters of the experimental groups, who were superior to the importers in their theme-list I accuracy scores, had *lower* I.Q. scores. However, this negative relationship between I.Q. and retention ability held only for those Ss who were selected for the second part of the experiment, the upper end of the total distribution. In the entire population a substantial positive correlation, $+.36$, was found between retention ability and I.Q.,[22]

---

[20] This difference achieves a t of 2.79 and is significant at the .02 level.

[21] *Biserial r* $= .12$, with a *C. R.* of 0.83, and is not significant. The question of the relationship between importation tendency and retention ability is also discussed above on p. 74.

[22] This correlation is significant beyond the .01 level. A negative relationship between I.Q. and importation tendency was also found (*biserial r* $= .21$), but it is too small and unreliable to attain statistical significance. The nonimporters in the total population achieved a higher mean I.Q. than the importers: 97.3 to 93.7 ($t = 1.17$), again not significant. Probably the main relationship is between I.Q. and retention ability, while importation relates to I.Q. only via its small negative relationship to retention ability.

corroborating the finding of a positive correlation between them in Experiment I.[23]

Table 13 shows that the original group (the group which later received the original version of the Ghost Story) and the explicated group of the importer chains earned almost identical theme-list I accuracy scores, and were also quite similar with respect to the amount of importation on theme list II and III. Of the nonimporters, however, the explicated group had a slight superiority over the original group in their theme-list I scores, and the original group showed a small edge in importations.

STEP 3. SERIAL REPRODUCTION OF THE TWO VERSIONS OF THE GHOST STORY, AND THE SECRETARY STORY

Seven days after the selection experiment, I administered the Ghost Story, in both its original and explicated versions, along with the Secretary Story,[24] to the lead-off members of the four chains. As in the Exploratory Experiment, I varied the order in which the stories were given: the No. 1 Ss received first the Ghost Story and second the Secretary Story; the No. 2's began with the Secretary Story; and so on. The No. 2's were tested in the afternoon of the same day that their predecessors were tested in the morning. The No. 3's were tested the following morning, No. 4's that afternoon, and No. 5's the following day.

At the end of each session I asked the Ss (using the standard instructions) to reproduce the theme list (theme list III in Table 13). After this I strongly urged them not to speak about the experiment to anyone until it was over.

Quantitative Results

I applied the same quantitative measures to the serial reproductions as in the foregoing experiments. In view of the fact that the present experiment was essentially a replication of the Exploratory Experiment (with the importation variable added and retention ability controlled), and since the Ss were secretaries in both cases, I analyzed the results from both experiments together wherever possible, in order to increase the precision of the statistical analyses. Tables 1 and 2 should be consulted for the raw data wherever such combined analyses are reported.

[23] See above, p. 74.
[24] The procedure was identical with that of the Exploratory Experiment; it is described above on p. 17.

1. ACCURACY ANALYSIS

Table 14 presents the theme score, the information score, and the word count of each of the serial reproductions. It reveals that the two stimulus variables made a conspicuous difference: the Secretary Story was better reproduced than either version of the Ghost Story, and the explicated version of the Ghost Story was superior to the original version.

It is interesting that both lead-off members of the importer chains did better than those of the nonimporter chains in their reproductions of the Secretary Story. In fact, in spite of their initial superiority in retention ability (on the selection tasks), the chains of nonimporters did no better than the chains of importers on the Secretary Story (although on the Ghost Story the nonimporters, on the whole, did better). This suggests that the familiarity factor may have benefited the importers more than it did the nonimporters. Moreover, the relationship between importation and explication that emerged in Experiment II (i.e., explication had a greater effect on nonimporters) did not appear here. In the present findings, explication affected importers as well as nonimporters.

The present analysis focuses on the effects of explication and familiarity upon accuracy of reproduction; therefore, in order to gain statistical precision, the results from the importer and nonimporter chains were pooled for the following accuracy analyses, and were studied in conjunction with the results from the Exploratory Experiment chains (see Tables 1 and 2).

Table 15 presents an analysis of the theme and information scores in each of the chains. The raw scores were converted into percentages based on the number of themes and information units in the original stimulus stories.[25] This analysis reveals the efficacy of familiarity and explication. The Secretary Story was superior to the Ghost Story on both measures of accuracy. The other variables attain statistical significance only on the information-score analyses, though the differences are all in the expected directions. The explicated version of the Ghost Story was superior to the original version, whereas there was no significant difference between the two groups of the Secretary Story.

[25] A similar analysis was done on the unconverted raw scores and yielded identical results.

Table 14

ACCURACY RESULTS OF THE ORIGINAL AND EXPLICATED VERSIONS OF THE GHOST STORY, AND THE SECRETARY STORY, BY IMPORTERS AND NONIMPORTERS

	Original group			Explicated group		
	Word Count	Theme Score	Information Score	Word Count	Theme Score	Information Score
Importers			Ghost Story			
Reproduction No. 1	175	15	55.5	244	21	76.5
Reproduction No. 2	104	9	26	206	18	50
Reproduction No. 3	89	8	23.5	149	13	34.5
Reproduction No. 4	60	6	14.5	117	11	25
Reproduction No. 5	37	5	11.5	107	10	17.5
Mean of Importer Chains	93.0	8.6	26.2	164.6	14.6	40.7
Nonimporters						
Reproduction No. 1	191	19	56	217	21	60
Reproduction No. 2	117	13	36.5	135	14	34.5
Reproduction No. 3	105	12	34	130	14	33.5
Reproduction No. 4	57	10	30	98	14	26
Reproduction No. 5	51	7	15.5	81	11	22
Mean of Nonimporter Chains	112.2	12.2	34.4	132.2	14.8	35.2
Mean of Ghost Chains	102.6	10.4	30.3	148.4	14.7	37.9

RETENTION STYLE AND RETENTION ABILITY 109

		Secretary Story			
Importers					
Reproduction No. 1	288	21	78.5	230	23	79
Reproduction No. 2	214	18	61	243	20	50
Reproduction No. 3	182	16	53	171	17	38.5
Reproduction No. 4	146	12	39.5	106	11	26
Reproduction No. 5	106	9	24.5	115	11	25
Mean of Importer Chains	187.2	15.2	51.3	173.0	16.4	43.7
Nonimporters					
Reproduction No. 1	248	19	74.5	233	22	75.5
Reproduction No. 2	145	15	43	194	20	56.5
Reproduction No. 3	127	14	36.5	190	19	48
Reproduction No. 4	108	13	34	154	15	40
Reproduction No. 5	115	11	33	140	14	36.5
Mean of Nonimporter Chains	148.6	14.5	44.2	182.2	18.0	51.3
Mean of Secretary Chains	167.9	14.9	47.8	177.6	17.2	47.5

Table 15

MEAN ACCURACY SCORES OF THE EXPLORATORY
EXPERIMENT AND EXPERIMENT III CHAINS,
COMPUTED AS PERCENTAGES BASED ON THE
STIMULUS STORIES

		Theme Score	Information Score
Ghost Story	Original Version	45.6	24.3
	Explicated Version	61.7	29.5
	Total	53.3	26.9
Secretary Story	O-Group	66.3	34.8
	E-Group	69.1	34.9
	Total	67.7	34.8
Experiment III Chains		58.3	39.9
Exploratory Experiment Chains		63.0	41.9

ANALYSIS OF VARIANCE

Source	D.F.	F-Ratio Theme	F-Ratio Information	P Theme	P Information
Stories	1:4	10.19	39.13	.05	> .01
Chains	1:4	1.14	95.13	—	> .01
Stories X Explication	1:3	3.85	156.4	—	> .01

A word-count analysis revealed that the reproductions of the Secretary Story were longer than those of the Ghost Story; that the reproductions of the explicated version were longer than those of the original versions; and that the reproductions of the importers were longer than those of the nonimporters. However, only the first of these findings attains statistical significance ($F = 7.60$, $d.f.$ of 1:4; significant at the .05 level).

I made a separate analysis of the first reproductions in each of the chains. Table 16 presents these results which, on the whole, are similar to those in Table 15, although only the information scores yield statistically significant differences. The Secretary Story was reproduced better than the Ghost Story from the start. It is noteworthy that, whereas the first member of the O-groups did better than those of the E-groups on the Secretary Story, on the Ghost Story it is the explicated version which was superior to the original version, indicating that it was the influence of the text rather than an initial superiority.

Several analyses of the final reproductions in each of the chains revealed that, while the above findings were all present in direction, only one of the differences attains statistical significance: the Secretary Story was reproduced better than both versions of the Ghost Story (for information score $F = 26.87$, $d.f.$ of 1:4; significant at the .01 level).

Analyses of all the reproductions on a successive stimulus basis also revealed that the explicated version fared better than the original version, and that the Secretary Story was retained better than either version of the Ghost Story. Moreover, this was also the case when only the last four reproductions of each chain were considered.

2. IMPORTATION ANALYSIS

Table 17 presents the importation score as well as the number of importations in each of the serial reproductions. It reveals, first, that the importers did more importing on both stories than the nonimporters did. A case-by-case comparison shows only one conspicuous case in which the reverse was true: the first member of the E-group (whose importations in the selection tasks, as shown in Table 13, were also quite low.) In spite of this case, the means for each chain clearly reflect the importation variable.

Table 16

MEAN ACCURACY SCORES OF THE NO. 1 REPRODUCTIONS, COMPUTED AS PERCENTAGES BASED ON THE STIMULUS STORIES

		Theme Score	Information Score
Ghost Story	Original Version	71.5	44.3
	Explicated Version	88.0	54.2
	Total	79.8	49.3
Secretary Story	O-Group	92.0	58.0
	E-Group	88.5	57.8
	Total	90.3	57.9
Experiment III Chains		85.0	50.9
Exploratory Experiment Chains		85.0	56.2

ANALYSIS OF VARIANCE

Source	D.F.	F-Ratio		P	
		Theme	Information	Theme	Information
Stories	1:4	3.29	10.87	—	> .05
Chains	1:3	—	28.25	—	> .05
Stories X Explication	1:3	2.99	25.13	—	> .05

Table 17
TOTAL NUMBER OF IMPORTATIONS AND TOTAL IMPORTATION SCORE OF EACH REPRODUCTION

	Ghost Story				Secretary Story				Total	
	Original version		Explicated version		Original group		Explicated group			
	Number	Score	Number	Score	Number	Score	Number	Score	Number	Score
Importers										
Reproduction No. 1	10	15	6	7	8	12	1	1		
Reproduction No. 2	10	14	5	8	4	5	4	7		
Reproduction No. 3	3	5	2	3	2	2	2	3		
Reproduction No. 4	4	4	6	10	2	1	3	6		
Reproduction No. 5	1	2	5	7	2	3	2	2		
Total Importer Chains	5.4	8.0	4.8	6.4	3.4	4.8	2.4	3.8	4.0	5.8
Nonimporters										
Reproduction No. 1	13	15	6	9	5	6	4	6		
Reproduction No. 2	6	8	7	8	3	3	4	5		
Reproduction No. 3	2	4	1	1	1	2	2	3		
Reproduction No. 4	2	4	1	2	0	0	0	0		
Reproduction No. 5	0	0	3	4	1	1	0	0		
Total Nonimporter Chain	4.6	6.2	3.6	4.8	2.0	2.4	2.0	2.8	3.1	4.1
Total	5.0	7.1	4.2	5.6	2.7	3.6	2.2	3.4		

The original version of the Ghost Story underwent more importations than did the explicated version, and this was true in the reproductions of both importers and nonimporters. However, since the importers of the O-group also did more importing on the Secretary Story, we cannot, on the basis of this finding alone, be sure that explication had a special effect on the amount of importing that the importers did. Nevertheless, in the case of the nonimporters, the fact that the E-group did slightly more importing on the Secretary Story and less on the explicated version of the Ghost Story does point to a special effect of explication. Therefore, we can conclude that, certainly for the nonimporters and probably for the importers, explication was inversely related to importation, in that explication diminished the amount of importation.

Finally, Table 17 shows that both versions of the Ghost Story underwent more importation than did the Secretary Story. Of the twenty possible comparisons of importation score as well as number of importations, in only three does the Secretary Story exceed the Ghost Story.

In order to make a comprehensive test of the importation variable, I made a statistical analysis of the importation scores of all the reproductions of the Ghost Story in Experiments II and III. This combined analysis, presented in Table 18, shows that the importation variable was highly significant—the importers did the most importing—and that the original version of the Ghost Story underwent significantly more importation than the explicated version.

Finally, I counted all the importations which occurred in the serial transmission chains of Experiments II and III. A comparison of the mean number of importations per chain, presented in Table 19, shows that the importers exceeded the nonimporters at a very high level of statistical significance.

3. REDUNDANCY ANALYSIS

Following the technique devised for the Exploratory Experiment, I assessed the redundancy of each serial reproduction. These results, presented in Table 20, are noteworthy first for the fact that they corroborate the main findings of the redundancy analysis from the Exploratory Experiment as presented in Table 3. The reproductions of each chain showed a fairly steady decline in the re-

Table 18

MEAN IMPORTATION SCORE ON THE GHOST STORY IN THE CHAINS OF EXPERIMENTS II AND III

Ghost Story	Original Version	5.9
	Explicated Version	4.5
Importers	Experiment III Chains	7.2
	Experiment II, Good Retainers	6.9
	Experiment II, Poor Retainers	5.4
	Total	6.5
Nonimporters	Experiment III Chains	5.4
	Experiment II, Good Retainers	2.1
	Experiment II, Poor Retainers	4.3
	Total	3.9

ANALYSIS OF VARIANCE

	D.F.	F-Ratio	P
Importation	1:7	17.19	> .01
Explication	1:7	5.87	> .05
Chains	2:7	3.46	—
Chains X Importation	2:2	199.25	> .01

Table 19

NUMBER OF IMPORTATIONS IN THE 28 CHAINS OF EXPERIMENTS II AND III

Groups	Mean	S.D.	t	P
Importers	17.1	4.3	3.45	< .01
Nonimporters	10.9	5.2		

dundancy indexes of both versions of the Ghost Story; but there was no comparable change in the redundancy indexes of the Secretary Story. Figure 1 shows the course of the redundancy indexes for the Ghost Story as a whole compared with that of the Secretary Story. The former shows a remarkably even and steady decline, while the latter is relatively flat.

The present study further confirmed the Exploratory Experiment in the finding that the original version of the Ghost Story suffered, in each of the two importer groups, a sharper decrease in redundancy than did the explicated version. It is also true that the differences between these two groups of reproductions were greater than the initial difference between the two versions of the stimulus story (which is 0.28). This was particularly true for the importers where the mean difference was 1.30, while for the nonimporters the mean difference was only 0.47.

The relationship between importation and redundancy is ambiguous. In their reproductions of the Secretary Story, the importers generally showed greater redundancy than the nonimporters. However, on the Ghost Story, the reverse was true. Figure 1 shows this graphically.

SUMMARY AND CONCLUSIONS

In this final experiment—a replication and integration of the foregoing ones—the main variables stood up well. The explicated version of the Ghost Story emerged from serial reproduction more intact than the original version, and the Secretary Story was much better recalled than either version of the Ghost Story. These find-

Table 20

REDUNDANCY ANALYSIS OF EACH REPRODUCTION

	Importers						Nonimporters					
	Original Group			Explicated Group			Original Group			Explicated Group		
	No. Lexical Units	Redundancy Score	Redundancy Index	No. Lexical Units	Redundancy Score	Redundancy Index	No. Lexical Units	Redundancy Score	Redundancy Index	No. Lexical Units	Redundancy Score	Redundancy Index
Ghost Story												
Reproduction No. 1	97	390	5.98	119	470	6.05	104	450	5.67	121	440	6.36
Reproduction No. 2	60	320	4.67	99	380	6.16	71	320	5.49	76	320	5.79
Reproduction No. 3	50	300	4.00	72	320	5.55	65	300	5.38	74	320	5.68
Reproduction No. 4	32	230	2.81	60	310	4.83	59	280	5.25	55	260	5.27
Reproduction No. 5	21	150	2.86	57	330	4.21	32	190	4.06	53	260	5.10
Mean of the Ghost Chains	52.0		4.06	80.1		5.36	66.2		5.17	75.8		5.64
Secretary Story												
Reproduction No. 1	125	520	5.84	113	490	5.66	108	540	5.00	113	470	5.84
Reproduction No. 2	102	450	5.59	94	430	5.43	71	380	4.65	96	390	5.94
Reproduction No. 3	91	410	5.50	73	320	5.61	62	340	4.52	92	340	6.30
Reproduction No. 4	66	270	5.91	52	250	5.19	56	330	4.19	74	270	6.35
Reproduction No. 5	48	250	4.79	53	230	5.66	49	270	4.49	73	260	6.44
Mean of the Secretary Chains	86.4		5.53	77.0		5.51	69.2		4.57	89.6		6.17

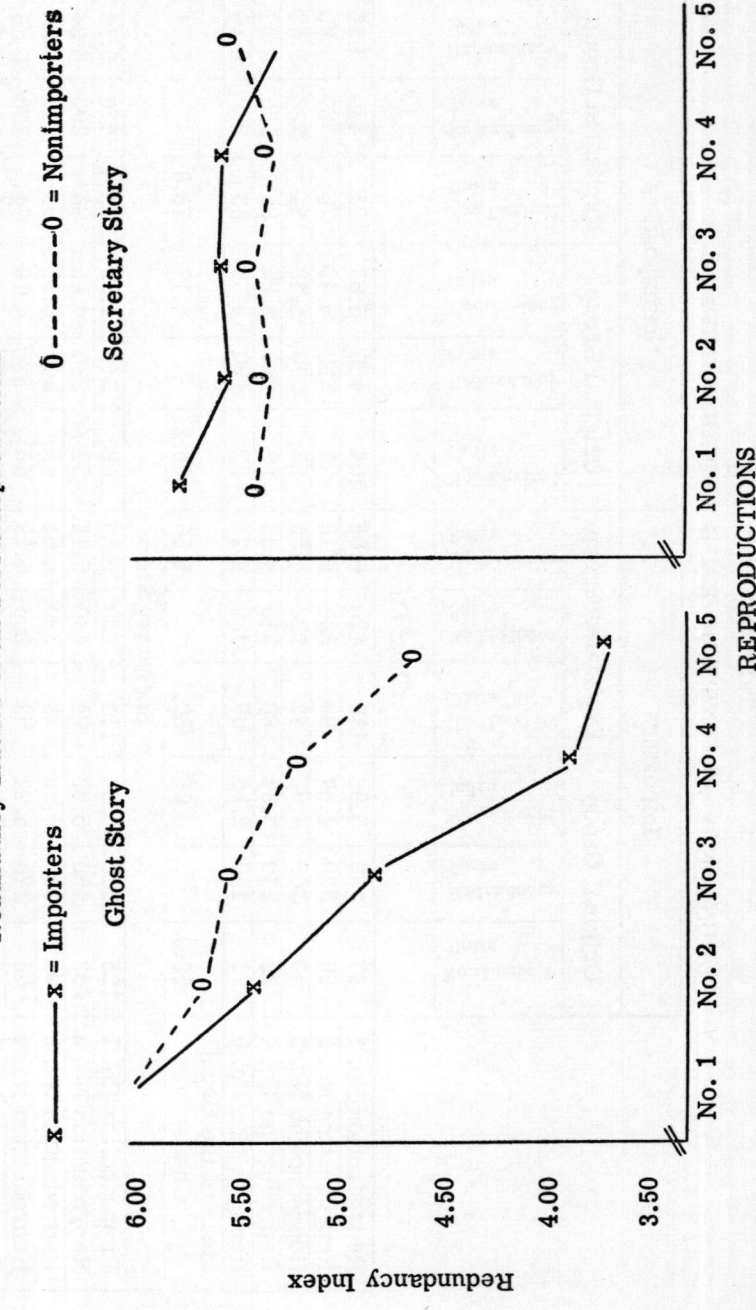

ings applied to the reproductions' accuracy and completeness as well as to their over-all redundancy structure. Moreover, the importation tendency proved once more to be a stable property of Ss. The importers (selected solely on the basis of the modified theme-list technique) consistently did more importing in their reproductions than the nonimporters did, justifying the designation of "importing" as a cognitive style, and lending support to the idea that recruitment is a basic schema process.

As in the earlier experiments, the original version of the Ghost Story underwent more importation than the explicated version. This finding was particularly conspicuous in the case of the nonimporters, though it also occurred to some extent among the importers. Moreover, as in the Exploratory Experiment, both versions of the Ghost Story underwent more importation than did the Secretary Story. These findings together suggest the following interpretation: when an organization of schemas is not adequate to deal with (i.e., interact with, integrate, and articulate) an extended experience, an intensification of the recruitment process occurs, resulting in recruitment from more or less related schemas. The Ghost Story, since it is largely unfamiliar and hence did not meet with adequate schema organizations in our Ss, gave rise to the importation of material more congruent with their schemas. This proposition can best be substantiated by directly examining the reproductions (see below, pp. 121-134).

The redundancy analysis of the present reproductions replicated the analysis made in the Exploratory Experiment, and reflected the differential collapse in structure of the stories: the original over the explicated version, and the Secretary over the Ghost Stories. The redundancy of the importers' reproductions was greater than those of the nonimporters, however, only in the case of the Secretary Story; this finding, paradoxically, did not emerge in the Ghost Story reproductions. The explanation may be that the importations, in the case of the alien Ghost Story, were unsuccessful because they failed to enhance redundancy. The detailed study of the reproductions may help to establish this relationship.

Because Experiment II showed that explication had a greater effect on nonimporters than on importers, I was led to propose that explicating and importing were overlapping or congruent functions. But in the present experiment, both explication and familiarity seemed to have had a greater facilitating influence on importers: the importers did better on the explicated than on the original version to a greater extent than did the nonimporters; and the importers (in spite of achieving lower accuracy scores in the selection task) did better on the Secretary Story than the nonimporters. So we have an important contradiction between the results of Experiments II and III. In one case the explications seem to have been *substitutive* with respect to importations, in the other they seem to have been *additive* or mutually facilitating.

The findings of Experiment III suggest an alternative interpretation of the relationship between explication and importation, one that focuses on the *fit* between text structure and schema structure rather than on the similarity between processes. The explicated and familiar material may have been easier for the importers to assimilate since it fitted in with their schema organization. It is as though they were more at home with stimulus material that was more like what they would do to it anyway; a highly explicated story suits their style and so is easier to apprehend and retain. However, further experimental exploration is necessary to determine under what conditions explication favors importers and when it favors nonimporters.

Qualitative Analysis

My examination of the serial reproductions in the Exploratory Experiment accomplished more than merely pointing up how much more coherent were the reproductions of the explicated version than of the original version of the Ghost Story, and how much more coherent than both of them were the Secretary Story reproductions. It revealed the pivotal integrating role played by explications: they closed gaps, formed transitions, solved contradictions, reduced ambiguity, and enhanced over-all coherence. Moreover, distortion and forgetting seemed to occur especially at those places where the original version contained gaps and ambiguities which my explicated version was designed to reduce—each of the serial reproductions seemed to tighten and reorganize the account around these points.

In addition, by tracing themes that were lost or conspicuously distorted somewhere along the chain, I could observe that they ". . . frequently followed a course of progressive contraction of content . . . gaps were opened and themes became disconnected and isolated . . . the pattern of skeletonization regularly included reshuffling of emphasis, rejuxtaposition of parts and relationships, and a steady tightening of structure around gaps and ambiguities, as well as a stripping away of redundant and ambiguous parts" (see p. 54). Many importations played a role that paralleled that of explications in that they also solved ambiguities and contradictions, and enhanced coherence—in fact, ". . . only those importations which were patently explicatory went on to influence subsequent reproductions" (see p. 55).

My detailed examination of the reproductions of Experiment III was undertaken first to see whether they concur with these observations and thus support the conclusions about schema functioning that I based on them; and second, to make a comparison between the importers' and the nonimporters' reproductions to see whether differences in their structure can be discerned that may teach us more about the role of importations.

My present examination will be briefer and more sketchy than it was in the Exploratory Experiment, since most of the ideas have already been spelled out there. The four chains of reproductions are presented below. The lettering of themes in all reproductions follows that of the theme analysis of the stimulus story,[26] and noteworthy changes, distortions, and importations are italicized. Following each chain's reproductions of the Ghost Story is its final (No. 5) reproduction of the Secretary Story.

EXPERIMENT III
SERIAL REPRODUCTION OF THE ORIGINAL VERSION OF THE GHOST STORY BY THE IMPORTERS

REPRODUCTION NO. 1

The War of the Ghost

a) Two men from Egulac *decided* to go up the river to hunt seals. *f*) They heard a *splash* and they saw a canoe coming toward them. *g*) "What do you think? We want to take you with us, *h*) we are going to war *with the Indians.*" *i*) "I will not go" said one of them. "My relatives *will* not know where I have gone." *j*) "But, you may go," he said turning to the other. *k*) So his *friend* went with the warriors and he returned home. *l*) They went up the river to a place called Kalama.

---

[26] The theme analysis of the Ghost Story is presented above on pp. 35-36.

Some returned *p*) *and he thought they were ghosts, but he was not frightened.* *m*) Many warriors were killed and *many injured.* *u*) The warrior went back and told of his great fight. *v*) "They said I was hit," he said, "but I didn't feel anything." He told his story and *then went to sleep.* In the morning the *people found him;* *w*) something black came out of his mouth, his face was contorted, *x*) the people stood up and cried. *y*) He was dead.

REPRODUCTION NO. 2
War *and* Ghosts

a) Some *hunters* were going up *to* Egulic to hunt seals. *f*) They heard a splash in the water and saw some *warriors* coming. *"What shall we do."* *i*) I can't go because my relative won't know where I am. *m*) Many warriors were killed but some returned *u*) and told of the great fight. *v*) "They said I was hit, but I don't feel hurt." After that the warrior went *back to* sleep. When morning came they found him *w*) with something black *sticking out* of his mouth, his face was *distorted.* *y*) He was dead. *p*) *The people thought the warriors who came back were ghosts.*

REPRODUCTION NO. 3
Warriors and Ghosts

a) Some men went to the Auglic to hunt seals. *f*) They heard a splash in the water and saw *many* warriors coming. *i*) "I can't join them because my relative will not know where I am." *m*) Many of the warriors were killed, but some returned *u*) to tell the story. *v*) "They said I was hit, but I don't feel hurt." The warrior went back to sleep. The next morning he was found *w*) with something black sticking out of his mouth, and his face *deformed.* *y*) The warrior was dead.

REPRODUCTION NO. 4

a) Some men went to the Auglic to hunt seals. *f*) They heard a splash in the water and saw warriors. *i*) "I can't come because my relatives won't know where I am." *v*) They *thought* I was hit, but it *didn't seem* to hurt. The warrior fell asleep. *When he awoke w*) there was a black thing in his mouth—*y*) he was dead.

REPRODUCTION NO. 5

a) Some men went to the Auglic to hunt. *f*) They heard a splash and there were warriors. *i*) "I can't come my relatives won't know." He was hit. *w*) *They found* a black thing in his mouth, *y*) he was dead.

REPRODUCTION NO. 5 OF THE SECRETARY STORY

Two sisters graduated from college. They both wanted to work in foreign countries so they could see the world. One sister was good in stenography and she got a job with a minister. *It was secrecy.* One day she came across a letter which said a city was to be bombed. Her sister lived in that city. She wanted to tell her sister, but she wanted to be loyal to the minister. *So she thought she would wait a few days and write to her and tell her to visit her.* Her sister started to walk to visit her and she met her sister on the road.

EXPERIMENT III
SERIAL REPRODUCTION OF THE ORIGINAL VERSION OF THE GHOST STORY BY THE NONIMPORTERS

REPRODUCTION NO. 1
Ghosts

a) One night two men went to the river *in* Egulac to hunt seals. *b*) It became *very* foggy. *c*) The men ceased their work. *d*) They heard *faint* war cries. *e*) They *quickly* headed toward shore and hid behind a log. *f*) They then heard the paddles of canoes. One canoe appeared in which there were five men. *g*) These men wished for a man to *help* fight. *i*) The first man did not wish to go, for, he said "I might be killed." This man who had not wanted to go returned home, *j*) after he said "You may go" to the other. *l*) Now these *six* men went up the river to Kalama to fight. *m*) They *came upon* the village and started *firing*. Many men from both sides were killed. *n*) The men shouted, *"Cease fire*, the Indian has been shot—*he is not sick."* s) This man now ventured toward home. *t*) He must tell everyone about his adventure, he thought. *u*) I was *fighting with ghosts* at Kalama when I was shot. *v*) I was not sick. When daylight came *w*) this man fell to the ground. A black substance was *pouring forth* from his mouth. *x*) People *called to him*. *y*) He was dead.

REPRODUCTION NO. 2

a) Two *hunters* were seal hunting in the river Egulac. *f*) They heard the paddle of canoes. *e*) They hid behind a log. They saw one canoe in which five men were. *g*) The man said they wanted *another* man to go to Kalamo and fight. *i*) The first *was afraid* and said, "I might be killed." He returned home, *j*) telling the other man, "You may go." *l*) The six men went to Kalamo *m*) and fought. *n*) Someone said, "Cease fire!" *"That Indian is not sick." When the first man left* he thought "I am not sick. *t*) I must tell my friends about fighting ghosts at Kalamo." *s*) When he arrived home he *lay down w*) with black *froth* coming from his mouth. *y*) He was dead.

REPRODUCTION NO. 3

a) Two hunters were hunting seals at the river Egulac. *f*) They heard the paddles of canoes. *e*) They hid behind a log. There were five men in the canoe. *g*) They wanted six men to come to Kalamo and fight. *i*) The first man said, "I may be killed," and he returned home, *j*) telling the other man, "You may go." *m*) The six men fought at Kalamo. *n*) Someone cried, "cease fire." "The Indian is not sick." "I am not sick," said the man. *t*) I must tell my friends about fighting ghosts at Kalamo. *s*) When he got home he lay down and *w*) black froth *foamed* from his mouth. *y*) He was dead.

REPRODUCTION NO. 4

a) Two men were hunting seals in the river Egulac. *f*) They heard the paddling of a canoe. *e*) They hid behind a log. There were five men in the canoe. *g*) They were going to fight at Kalamo. *i*) "I am not going," said one man, "*I will die.*" "The Indian *is sick.*" "I am not sick," said the man. So he went home. *m*) The other six men went to Kalamo to fight. *t*) "I am going home to tell the people about fighting the ghosts at Kalamo." *s*) He went home, lay down and *w*) black foamed at his mouth. *y*) Then he died.

REPRODUCTION NO. 5

f) They heard the paddling of a canoe. *e*) They hid behind log. There were five men in the canoe. The Indian is sick. *i*) "I am not going I will die." *g*) They were going to fight at *s*) He went home. When he reached home *w*) black froth foamed at his mouth. *y*) Then he died.

REPRODUCTION NO. 5 OF THE SECRETARY STORY

Two sisters who graduated from a business college at Massar decided to become foreign secretaries so they could see the world together. They promised to write to their mother often. One sister who was a competent secretary, got a job with a prime minister. "You must always be loyal," the prime minister said, "because many important documents pass through this office." One day a declaration of war from another nation passed through the office where the girl was working. She decided to walk to that nation which was only twelve kilometers away to warn her sister. When she got there, her sister was already there to warn her. The next day both nations were destroyed.

EXPERIMENT III

SERIAL REPRODUCTION OF THE EXPLICATED VERSION OF THE GHOST STORY BY THE NONIMPORTERS

REPRODUCTION NO. 1

The War *with* the Ghosts

a) One night two men from the *city* of Euglac went fishing down by the river. *b*) The night was foggy and *dark.* *c*) *A good night* for ghosts. *d*) As they were fishing they heard sounds of a war party. *e*) They tried to hide *f*) but they could not and one of the canoes came straight up to them. *h*) "We are going to fight," they said. *g*) "You *are* going with us." *i*) One man said he couldn't go because he had a family *to take care of,* *j*) but he said to the other, "You go, *there is no one waiting for you.*" *k*) So one man went with the party and one went home. When they reached the *city* of Kalama *m*) they began to fight. *n*) Then someone shouted, "We better go, the Indian is shot." *q*) I did not feel any pain but they said I was shot. *r*) That was because when you are with ghosts at night you feel no pain. Many people were killed and *a great number injured. Yet, the Indian felt no pain.* *s*) When the man went home to Euglac u) he told the people he went fighting with the ghosts, v) and that he was shot but had felt no pain. w) Then the man fell, something black rolled out of his mouth. x) The people all got up and cried. y) He was dead.

REPRODUCTION NO. 2

a) One day two men were fishing *in the Euglac River*. b) The night was dark and foggy. c) It was a good night for ghosts. d) Suddenly they *saw* a *group* of canoes. One canoe was heading toward them. h) "We have come to fight. g) You *must* come with us." i) "But I have a *wife* and family," said one man. j) "You have no one, you go." l) They went to the city of Kalama. m) There they fought. q) *One man was wounded*, but he did not feel it. That was because he was fighting *with* Indians. Many *Indians* were killed and a great number wounded. But the man felt no pain. s) He went back to his town in Euglac and v) said to *his* people, "I have been shot, but I feel no pain." He then fell to the ground. y) He was dead.

REPRODUCTION NO. 3

a) One day two men were fishing in the Euglac River. b) It was dark and foggy. c) It was a good night for ghosts. d) Suddenly they saw a group of canoes. One canoe was coming toward them. h) "We are going to fight. g) Come with us!" i) "I have a wife and family," said one man. j) "You have no one. You go." l) They went to *the* Kalama m) to fight. q) One man got wounded but he could not feel the pain. This was because he was fighting with Indians. Many Indians were wounded and dead but the man couldn't feel the pain of his wound. s) He went back to the Euglac *River* where he lived and v) he told everyone, "I have been wounded, but I cannot feel the pain." He fell to the ground. y) He was dead.

REPRODUCTION NO. 4

a) Two men were fishing on the Eglac River. b) It was dark and foggy. c) It was a good night for Ghost. d) They saw canoes coming toward them. *They were Indians.* g) "Come h) we are going to fight." i) "*No* I have a family. j) You have none. You go." l) They went to the Kalamac m) to fight. q) The man was wounded but could not feel the pain because they were fighting Indians. A lot of Indians were wounded and dead. s) The man went home. v) He said, "I am wounded but I can not feel the pain." Then he dropped. y) The man was dead.

REPRODUCTION NO. 5

a) Two men went fishing on the Eglac River. b) It was dark and foggy. *Then a ghost came.* d) They saw *boats* coming. They were Indians. l) They went to the Kalamac *River*. m) They came to fight. h) They said, "We are going to fight. i) No I have a family. j) You have none. You go." Many Indians were wounded and dead. q) The man was wounded but did not feel pain because he was fighting the Indians. s) When he went home v) he said he was wounded but didn't feel pain.

REPRODUCTION NO. 5 OF THE SECRETARY STORY

There were two sisters. Business school graduates. They said to their mother one day, we are going to a foreign country to work. This way we can see the world and work at the same time. One sister worked for a foreign minister. They decided to write to each other every day. One sister worked for a minister. One day he said to her you are working for me. You should be loyal to me. He told her of an attack of a city. She remembered that, that was the city her sister was working in. She decided to write to her sister but then remembered her loyalty. She wouldn't write but her sister would think she was sick. She didn't get a letter from her sister the next day. She went to see if she was sick. They met halfway. The next day both cities were bombed because both had planned an attack.

EXPERIMENT III
SERIAL REPRODUCTION OF THE EXPLICATED VERSION OF THE GHOST STORY BY THE IMPORTERS

REPRODUCTION NO. 1
The War of the Ghost

a) Two men of Eluca went fishing one night. *b*) While they were there the *air* became foggy and calm. *c*) Then they *remembered* it was the omen of *the ghost*. *d*) They heard some cries *that were like war cries* and *e*) ran to the shore to hide behind a log. *f*) But they could not hide from these canoes. One canoe came right toward them. It had five men in it. *h*) They told the men that they were going to a *town outside of Kalama* to fight *g*) and they wanted them to go. *i*) One of the men said, "I can't go. I have not told my relatives where I am. *j*) But you" he said to the other man "have no relatives. You can go." *k*) So the man went with them. *l*) When they reached the shore the people *were there* and *m*) they began to fight. Many people were killed. *n*) Then he heard one of the men say, "That Indian has been hurt, we must leave." *o*) His fellows had never called him an Indian *q*) and he felt no pain. *r*) Then he remembered that when you are in the company of the ghost you feel no pain as long as the night last. *s*) When he got back he started a fire to summon the people. *u*) He told them of his *experience* and how many *of their people* had been killed. *w*) In the morning he fell, something black came from his mouth. His face was contorted. *y*) He was dead.

REPRODUCTION NO. 2

a) Two men from Eluca were *out in a boat* fishing when *b*) the *sea* became foggy and calm. *c*) They remembered that *when the ocean became like this* it was the omen of the ghost *to appear*. *d*) They saw some men coming in a *boat* and *e*) they went to shore and hid behind a log. *It was a canoe that they had seen* and there were five men in it. *h*) The men told the two men that there *was a war going on* at Kalama and *g*) they wanted *their help*. *i*) One man said that he had relatives and *they were expecting him back home. j) The men turned to the other fellow and said,* "You have no relatives, come with us." *k)* He left with the five men and *m)* began to battle at the place spoken about. *He became wounded* and *n)* the *five men* said, *"Let us take this Indian away,* he is wounded." *q)* The man could feel no pain and *r)* he remembered that the night you were with the ghost you felt no pain. *s)* He got back to *his* people and *u)* told them that many of their people had been killed at the battle. *w)* The next morning something black came from his mouth. His face was contorted. *y)* He was dead.

REPRODUCTION NO. 3

a) There were two men fishing in a boat when *b)* the sea got foggy and *stormy. c)* The men had *always heard* that when the sea got that way a ghost would appear. *e)* The men *rushed back* to land and hid behind a log. *d)* They saw a canoe coming with five men in it. The men came up to them and *h)* told them that there was a war going on in Kalama and *g)* they *needed* help. *i)* One of the men said that his relatives were expecting him home. *j)* The men from the canoe told the other man that he had no relatives and that he was to come with them. The man was wounded in the battle *s)* and went home and *u)* told his people that many of their people were dead. *w)* The next morning they found the man with something black coming out of his mouth. *y)* The man was dead.

REPRODUCTION NO. 4

a) There were *three* men fishing in a boat one day when *b)* the sea became foggy and stormy. *c)* The men had *been told* that when the sea gets stormy a ghost appears. *They became frightened e)* and went into shore and hid behind a *large rock. d)* Soon a boat with some men in it came *into the island* and *h)* they told the fisherman that there was a war on Kamara. They were going and *k)* they took the man with no relatives with them. When the fighting was over *s)* one of them went home and *u)* told his *family* that *all their relatives* had been killed. *w)* Next morning they found him with black stuff coming out of his mouth. *y)* He was dead.

REPRODUCTION NO. 5

a) There were three *fishermen* in a boat when *b)* the sea *started to get* foggy and stormy. *c)* They were told that whenever the sea gets stormy a *big white* ghost appears. *e)* They went ashore and hid behind a large rock.

d) Some men came to the island in a boat. *h)* They said that a war *had started* on Karma, *and that they were taking all single men with them.* After the fighting was over *s)* one man went back to his family and *u)* told them that all of their relatives had been killed. *He got up* the next morning, *w)* black rolled out of his mouth and *y)* he fell dead.

REPRODUCTION NO. 5 OF THE SECRETARY STORY

There were two girls who went to Europe after graduating from business college. One worked for the Ambassador of Maintailin. She wrote her sister letters. The Ambassador told her not to write anything about his business in her letters. One day she found a letter on his desk that said the city in which her sister lived was going to be bombed. She had already written some letters to her sister so she couldn't write any more. So she decided to walk to see her sister because she was only fifteen kilometers away. So she walked to her sister and met her *in the middle of* the path while their two countries were being bombed.

1. IMPORTERS' REPRODUCTIONS OF THE ORIGINAL VERSION OF THE GHOST STORY

Reproduction No. 1 is a rather poor account of the story, and, even though it achieves a high importation score (see Table 18), it is quite disconnected, especially the first half of it. Nevertheless, it is not as disconnected as its counterpart, the nonimporters' reproduction No. 1 of the original version, which, in spite of achieving the same high importation score, has a lower redundancy index (see Table 20). This suggests that here the importers' importations enhanced redundancy to a somewhat greater extent than nonimporters' importations.

The major importations, in the present case, cluster in the second half of the story, whereas the first part suffers more from theme loss [themes *b*) and *c*) are wholly absent]. Theme *g*) enters abruptly and fails to indicate who made the INVITATION. After theme *l*), WAR-TRIP, the account becomes confused: there is no RETREAT, REALIZATION is confused, and "he was not sick" is transformed to "he was not frightened," thereby leveling the ENIGMA. Also conspicuous are the change from "rested" to "went to sleep," and the importations "splash" and "the people found him."

The title of reproduction No. 2, "War and Ghosts," hints that this account has lost the point of the story. Theme *p*), the important REALIZATION, is merely tacked on at the end, just as in the original version reproductions in the Exploratory Experiment. Here, however, it is not wholly disconnected; this *S* tries to make sense of the ghost element by means of a major importation that integrates the ghost idea into the body of the story: "The people thought the warriors who came back were ghosts." This is strikingly explicationlike or rationalized (in Bartlett's sense).

The first half of reproduction No. 2 is highly fragmented, and a marked decrease in accuracy and redundancy is apparent—six additional themes are lost, and, in spite of a high importation score, its redundancy index dips to 4.67. In this case, therefore, the importations fail to sustain the account's redundancy. Themes g) and h), INVITATION and WAR-PLANS, both drop out completely, perhaps because of the abrupt way they were introduced in the previous reproduction, and the ambiguity that lay in their being enclosed in quotation marks yet not attributed to any actor. The importation "what shall we do" is interesting because it seems, more than anything else, to express this S's perplexity with the story.

In spite of the bad beginning, in the post-BATTLE part of the story this S begins to tie things together and make some sense out of the confusion in her stimulus story. For example, she introduces conjunctions to organize the material: "many were killed *but* some returned *and* told . . ." This use of conjunctions (which, incidentally, the redundancy analysis fails to capture) was most characteristic of the importers.

Although the title of reproduction No. 3 connects the "warriors" with the "ghosts," the body of the account fails to include this idea. In fact, it makes no mention of ghosts at all. Aside from this loss of theme p), REALIZATION, there is no further theme loss in this reproduction, and, on the whole, it seems to tighten up the account somewhat. The importation "what shall we do"—which did not seem to serve any purpose in No. 2 except to reflect the S's perplexity—drops out.

Reproduction No. 4 further abbreviates the account. The remnants of theme m), the BATTLE, drop out (the only allusion to any fighting in No. 3 was "many of the warriors were killed"). Similarly theme u), REVELATIONS, which had become a minor issue in No. 3, is squeezed out entirely. The title also drops out; it had ceased to have a relation with the story since REALIZATION was missing. A striking contradiction occurs at the end: "he awoke" is followed by "he was dead." It would be surprising indeed if this strange sequence survived in the subsequent reproduction.

In reproduction No. 5 theme v), the ENIGMA, drops out. In No. 4 it was certainly incongruous since, although "it didn't seem to hurt," he died nonetheless. In No. 5, S simply accepts that he must have been hit. On the whole, this account is only a remnant of the story—compare it with this S's reproduction of the Secretary

Story. It is striking how relatively well the Secretary Story survived serial reproduction and how well the redundancy analysis reflected this differential collapse (see Table 20).

2. NONIMPORTERS' REPRODUCTION OF THE ORIGINAL VERSION OF THE GHOST STORY

The lead-off member of the nonimporter chain gives a more accurate and complete reproduction of the original version than does the lead-off member of the importer chain, and it undergoes the same degree of importation. Nevertheless, a stylistic difference is clearly detectable that corresponds to its lower redundancy index. Notice how staccato and choppy the account is, how much shorter are its sentences, how abrupt its flow. On the whole, the nonimporters tended toward a sparer, more telegraphic style even where they imported. This characteristic did not always show up, as it did in the present case, in the redundancy analysis.

In reproduction No. 1 theme h), WAR-PLANS, is missing, as is theme p), the vital REALIZATION. Theme n), the RETREAT, is stated along with part of the ENIGMA, but in a very disconnected and ambiguous way that led to difficulties in subsequent reproductions.

The choppiness of No. 1 is also conspicuous in No. 2. Just as in the importers' reproductions of the original version, themes b) and c), ATMOSPHERE and SOMETHING UP, are dropped completely. (These ambiguous and gappy themes were ones that I had explicated in the explicated version.) Theme d), WAR-CRIES, also drops out. These three themes were stated very abruptly with no preparation or redundancy in No. 1, and this may have contributed to their present loss. The BATTLE episode is sharply abbreviated here, and theme n), the RETREAT, is changed in such a way as to reduce the confusion created in No. 1: the shooting of the Indian is omitted completely and the ENIGMA is separated off and repeated. Finally, theme x), the REACTION OF THE PEOPLE, which in No. 1 was transformed from "cried" to "called to him," drops out.

Reproduction No. 3 is a very faithful reproduction of No. 2; remarkably little is lost and nothing is added. Only one information unit is changed: "coming" becomes the more graphic "foamed."

Aside from the rather incongruous displacement of theme m), the BATTLE, reproduction No. 4 is a fairly good account of its predecessor, although its relationship to the Ghost Story itself is rather tenuous. The RETREAT drops out, and what remains is a concentration on the ENIGMA in the form of a debate as to whether "the Indian is sick" or not.

In reproduction No. 5 the opening theme drops out, as does theme v), REVELATIONS. (In No. 4 the latter, instead of appearing in a separate sentence as it did earlier, had become reduced to a minor part of the "going home" decision.) Theme m), BATTLE, also drops out, perhaps because of the confusing way in which it was displaced in No. 4 following its marked abbreviation in No. 2. This final reproduction of the chain is a very choppy and disconnected account in which the original story (or, in fact, any story at all) is hardly discernible. On the other hand, how coherent and relatively complete an account of the Secretary Story this No. 5 S gives!

It may be emphasized that, aside from the occurrence of importations, stylistic differences between importers and nonimporters were observable. The importers showed more importation; this did not, however, result in superior reproductions nor did it consistently enhance their redundancy indexes. It should be borne in mind that the two groups were not equal in retention ability—the nonimporters were clearly superior.

3. THE NONIMPORTERS' REPRODUCTIONS OF THE EXPLICATED VERSION OF THE GHOST STORY

Reproduction No. 1 of the explicated version by the nonimporter chain gives a quite complete, accurate, and coherent account of the story—much better than either lead-off member of the original version. It is interesting to observe that this nonimporter abbreviates and condenses and that the abbreviations and condensations occur largely in the themes that I had explicated: e.g., theme c), the OMEN, is reduced to "a good night for ghosts," and theme r), the PROTECTION, is similarly cut down. This account loses theme l), WAR-TRIP (which, however, it implies so well that it returns in reproduction No. 2, theme t), DECISION TO TELL, and theme p), REALIZATION, which drops out cleanly, leaving a gap at that point in the story.

Reproduction No. 2 markedly reduces the story and gives quite a choppy account of it—its sentences are conspicuously brief. This is only partly revealed in the extent of its redundancy-index loss (6.36 to 5.79). This reproduction also contains quite a few importations, but they fail to alleviate its choppiness or enhance its redundancy. Theme e), HIDING, drops out (in No. 1, instead of commanding its own sentence, it had become connected with a long sentence: "they tried to hide but could not and . . ."). Theme n), the RETREAT, is omitted, PROTECTION idea of theme r) is essentially lost, and the ghosts are changed to Indians.

Reproduction No. 3 is an almost word-perfect replica of No. 2, loses no thematic material, maintains the redundancy index, and contains only one minor importation. A few minor changes in it will be mentioned below, because they seem to have had interesting consequences in Nos. 4 and 5.

Like No. 3, reproduction No. 4 loses no thematic material, but it tells the story in a more telegraphic way, omitting some redundancies—e.g., the repetition of the ENIGMA between themes q) and s). There is an interesting importation at the beginning: "they were Indians." Apparently this is S's attempt to deal with the fact that, although the ghost element is introduced in the OMEN, the previous reproduction does not speak of ghosts again. The ghost omen therefore can only be explained as a kind of false alarm, and this is apparently what S thought, since the importation, coming right after the OMEN, implies "(but they were not ghosts) they were Indians."

The final reproduction is quite confused. It loses only three themes, but they are important ones: theme c), OMEN, theme g), INVITATION, and theme y), DEATH. The first one is replaced by a conspicuously disconnected distortion, "then a ghost came." This may partly result from the fact that No. 4 had written "ghost" in the singular ("it was a good night for ghost"), which is hard to understand. The INVITATION drops out via an interesting sequence of progressive contraction, so common in the Exploratory Experiment's reproductions: in No. 1, "you are going with us"; in No. 2, "you must come with us"; in No. 3, "come with us!"; in No. 4, simply "come . . ."; No. 5 merely goes one step further. Finally, it is instructive to compare this No. 5 reproduction with that of the Secretary Story, which is much more complete and coherent and achieves a very high redundancy index (6.44).

4. THE IMPORTERS' REPRODUCTIONS OF THE EXPLICATED VERSION OF THE GHOST STORY

Even though inferior in retention ability to begin with, the lead-off member of this chain gives the best reproduction of all, not only attesting to the efficacy of explication, but also indicating that explication had a greater effect upon importers. This is a faithful rendition of the story, a flowing narrative with many connectives retained and many added. "Ghosts" is made singular throughout —"the ghost." It seems that, for this S, the Indians are not equated with the ghosts, but rather the ghost is somehow *with* the men. This interpretation would have been contradicted by the line in the stimulus story "oh, they surely are ghosts" which represents the REALIZATION theme, and so this theme is omitted from the reproduction. The account also loses theme v), ENIGMA REPEATED, and theme x), REACTION OF PEOPLE. Theme o), the "INDIAN," though retained, is essentially disconnected, and a gap has been created here. It is not surprising that this theme quickly becomes lost.

Reproduction No. 2 contains many importations and changes, yet the line and sense of the story are well preserved and the structure of the account is even more coherent than its stimulus (the redundancy index rises from 6.05 to 6.16, the only instance in which a Ghost Story reproduction showed an increase in redundancy). Many of its importations seem to add emphasis (as was also true of the lead-off member of the explicated group in the Exploratory Experiment, who was so conspicuously an importer); others serve to tighten the connections of the themes. For example, in theme c), OMEN, "it" (from No. 1) is expanded to "when the ocean became like this," and "to appear" is added to "the ghost"; in theme i), REFUSAL, "I have not told my relatives where I am" (from No. 1) is probably considered too weak and so it is changed to a stronger excuse, "they were expecting him back home"; the RETREAT is expanded from "we must leave" to "let us take this Indian away, he is wounded." Theme l), WAR-TRIP, is lost (in No. 1 it had been reduced to a clause of the BATTLE). Finally, as expected, "INDIAN," theme o), which was so disconnected anl ambiguous in No. 1, drops out.

Reproduction No. 3 loses a number of themes, but, aside from the RETREAT and ENIGMA parts of the story, it remains a rather good account. In theme b), ATMOSPHERE, an interesting transformation occurs: "calm" becomes its opposite, "stormy." This S apparently associates storm rather than calm with a bad omen. "*The* ghost" (of No. 2) becomes "*a* ghost" and then ceases to figure in the story. The BATTLE episode is reduced to one statement about the man getting wounded, and theme q), the ENIGMA, is dropped. It is difficult to understand this major loss except in the light of the fact that it is often this portion of the story for which these Ss are least likely to have appropriate schemas.

More importations are introduced in reproduction No. 4: a third man is added; "they became frightened" is added (this S's schema apparently dictates that people are afraid of ghosts); and an "island" is introduced in the ocean. Theme g), INVITATION, which had become quite minor in the previous reproductions, drops out, and with it goes theme h), REFUSAL.

Aside from two changes, reproduction No. 4 is well preserved in No. 5. The ghost becomes "a big white" one (white is, after all, the color of ghosts), and "they took the man with no relatives" from No. 4 becomes "they were taking all single men." On the whole, however, the story is still discernible in this final reproduction, though it is not as intact as the Secretary Story is.

SUMMARY AND CONCLUSIONS

On the whole, direct examination of these reproductions revealed many of the same phenomena as did the Exploratory Experiment and supported many of its conclusions. The following five general conclusions may be drawn from the present examination.

1. Explication and familiarity clearly proved to be effective variables: both original version chains underwent a rapid and conspicuous collapse in content and structure, while the explicated versions remained comparatively intact. A comparison with the final reproductions of the Secretary Story highlighted this difference, and at the same time showed how much more accurate and coherent than both were the Secretary Story reproductions.

2. The reproductions of nonimporters and importers were stylistically different: the former were generally leaner in structure,

more disconnected, and more abbreviated than those of the importers; the latter seemed more continuous and coherent. The redundancy analysis sometimes failed to reflect this difference, a failure which seems largely due to the fact that it does not deal adequately with conjunctions and connecting clauses. The use of conjunctions was most characteristic of the importers.

3. A high importation score did not always result in increased connectedness and coherence. However, importation increased redundancy more for the importers than it did for the nonimporters. This finding suggests that importers' importations differ from nonimporters' in that they enhance structural coherence. This corresponds to the finding that some importations seemed like explications, others did not. The importers' importations in the explicated version chain for the most part resembled explications (and thereby seemed to facilitate understanding and retention); in the original version their importations were less like explications (e.g., the importation that merely expressed S's perplexity), and therefore often failed to cement the story by reducing gaps and ambiguities, and enhancing redundancy. Their importations sometimes leveled away an important theme (e.g., the ENIGMA theme). Paradoxically, it was the nonimporters' importations which, though they were less frequent, most often seemed truly like explications.

The originally gappy and ambiguous themes were, as in the Exploratory Experiment, the main loci of distortion and loss. It was interesting to observe that, in the explicated version, my explications were abbreviated and condensed *by the nonimporters*. On the other hand the importers seemed to use my explications to good advantage, and their reproductions benefited and were superior to the nonimporters'. This supports the idea of a congruence between the explicated version and the importers' schema functioning that facilitated their assimilation of the story, and accounts for the fact that explication benefited the importers more than the nonimporters.

4. Many of the importations and transformations in the present reproductions seemed clearly to reveal and express the Ss' personal schemas in terms of their understanding of the events in the story based upon their own conceptions and experiences. This occurred more frequently and much more flagrantly than it did in the Ex-

ploratory Experiment. Perhaps this was due to the fact that the Ss were younger and less sophisticated; hence they relied more on recruitment in their schema formation and functioning, and were less critical of their own cognitions. For the same reasons, perhaps, it was more characteristic of the present chains that peripheral and unrelated material, contradictions and incongruous sequences, quickly dropped out.

5. The sequences of thematic loss following progressive contractions of content, shifts in emphasis and rejuxtaposition of themes, creation of ambiguities and opening of gaps, were conspicuous, and followed the same pattern as in the Exploratory Experiment.

4
CONCLUSIONS AND IMPLICATIONS

This study opened with three broad questions: (1) What processes underlie people's reproductions of a story? (2) Which properties of stories facilitate and hinder recovery? (3) Do people differ systematically in the way they retain and reproduce stories? The experiments reported in Chapter 3, taken together with the Exploratory Experiment, permit some answers. This closing chapter, which is organized into three parts according to the three questions, summarizes the main findings, formulates a number of general conclusions and tentative hypotheses set in the theoretical framework that guided the research, and discusses further lines of research. Like the Discussion and Conclusions section of Chapter 2, it also reviews some relevant literature and takes up some theory.

Properties Facilitating and Hindering Remembering

Explication, familiarity, and coherence emerge as the main stimulus variables in this study. All three proved to facilitate learning and remembering; their absence led to fragmentation, distortion, and forgetting.

The serial reproduction findings suggest that familiarity exerted a greater facilitating effect than did explication. Familiarity with content was most effective in maintaining structural coherence even when it did not prevent substantial loss of content. Moreover, it occasioned less importation and fewer transformations. On the other hand, explication could not prevent the eventual decline of structural coherence, though it did significantly slow its rate. Explication also occasioned less importation and transformation than did the gappy and ambiguous original stimulus. These findings suggest the following theoretical propositions:

1. When a stimulus experience creates a schema organization which is made up of already well-articulated and stable schemas, that schema organization is likely to be well structured and stable (in that it can function to reconstruct the experience more completely, accurately, and coherently; and it does so with less recruitment of extraneous schemas and less transformation of its parts).

2. Schemas which are already present in the individual assure an adequate schema organization, and are more effective than those which have to be mobilized by explicatory links in the stimulus material; i.e., when a schema organization depends upon explications, it has less chance of surviving than if it depends on already present schemas. Nevertheless, such explicatory links go far in assuring an adequate schema organization.

Do explications function by inserting familiar material at unfamiliar and ambiguous places? Is explication wholly a matter of promoting familiarity, or does another factor also underlie its effectiveness as a focus of schema influence? It seems valid to view explication from a structural vantage and to propose that, by reducing gaps or discontinuities, explications enhance connectedness and thereby enhance *meaningfulness*. For, according to many theorists, connectedness is an essential ingredient in meaningfulness. Perhaps a brief digression will sharpen this point.

Learning theorists have, in general, viewed meaningfulness in terms of familiarity, i.e., previous learning which results in associations and expectations. Miller and Selfridge (1950), for example, argue that ". . . the significant distinction is not to be drawn between meaning and nonsense, but between materials that utilize previous learning and permit positive transfer and materials that do not . . . meaningful material is easy to learn, not because it is meaningful per se, but because it preserves the short-range associations that are familiar to the Ss" (p. 183).

However, there is an important difference between such meaningful material as poetry and prose, which have been found to yield relatively small amounts of retroactive inhibition (McGeoch and McKinney, 1934), and lists of discrete meaningful words, which paradoxically give rise to a great deal of interference (Mc-

Geoch and McDonald, 1931; McGeoch and McGeoch, 1936).[27] Newman (1939) concluded, from these findings as well as from his own research, that what is crucial here is the factor of *connectedness*. He rejects such associationistic notions as "verbal pigeonhole" and verbal trace system, and contends that ". . . some concept other than that of associations, bonds, identical elements or the like must be supplied . . . such a concept would require that meaning reside in the structure of organization of the material to be learned, in the organized 'sense' of the story, in a 'context' of meaning which does not consist of indifferent bonds" (1939, p. 70). In other words, meaning is largely a function of the structure of a stimulus experience, with connectedness as its major condition.

This formulation fits well with my findings that when a stimulus story starts out with major gaps, content and structure soon collapse. Such a story also gives rise to efforts on the part of Ss to recruit material to forestall this collapse. To the extent that S has appropriate schemas at his disposal, his attempt will be successful. If he is without them, then his attempts may entail considerable fractionation.

Experimentation on this proposition can take the form of using as Ss experts with varying amounts of knowledge relevant to a stimulus situation.[28] A relevant study would be to examine differences among Ss with equivalent knowledge and interests to see along what other parameters their schema functioning still varies: are there differences in recruitment and fractionation, in stability and coherence? A second experimental approach, which I have recently used, is to try to teach Ss about a relevant topic—to make them expert—to see whether and how such knowledge affects their

---

[27] A recent experiment by Postman and Rau (1957), comparing the recall of lists of nonsense syllables and lists of words, failed to find any difference between them when differential rate of acquisition (words were learned faster than nonsense syllables) was taken into account. The conclusion was that ". . . it appears that nonsense materials are retained at least as well as are meaningful materials. In fact, there are strong indications that free recall is higher for nonsense syllables than for meaningful words" (1957, p. 266).

[28] Allport and Postman found that proper names tended to be leveled out except that ". . . if the Ss' interest or training predisposes them to pay especial attention to proper names, these may be retained" (1947, p. 61). I have recently carried out an experiment which demonstrates this point and at the same time shows the influence of already present highly developed schemas on selective recall.

retention. In view of the fact that I conceive of schemas as concepts rather than as elements of content, in my experiment I taught the Ss concepts rather than contents. One of my expectations was that such concepts would enhance connectedness more than content would.

One of the structural variables that emerged in the present studies is lexical redundancy, which is an index to connectedness. That redundancy plays an important role is reflected in the finding that importations (particularly those that were explicatory) served to enhance redundancy. Moreover, it seemed at times to be specifically the redundancy rather than the fact of explication that was efficacious in inviting importation. The explicated version of the Ghost Story underwent less importation, but the explicated version of the Potlatch Story underwent more. The fact that my explication of these stories had the opposite effect, in the former case increasing redundancy and in the latter case decreasing it, seems to have been the crucial factor. In both cases, it was the less redundant version that suffered more importation. Since redundancy proved to reflect coherence, in which connectedness is an essential ingredient, these findings may simply reflect the fact that many importations served to enhance connectedness and, in that sense, meaningfulness.

Processes Underlying Reproductions of a Story

There was ample evidence in the present findings of the active schema processes which Bartlett considered so important. There was evidence of "rationalization," of "effort after meaning," and of "fit," which seemed directed by the Ss' preconceptions and attitudes (and, I would add, their styles). Many importations, transformations, rejuxtapositions, and changes of emphasis clearly fell into these categories. However, many, if not all, of these changes might also be conceptualized in the Gestalt terms of leveling, sharpening, and assimilation.

These three Gestalt categories were sufficient for Allport and Postman (1947) to classify the changes they found when they transmitted rumors verbally. Their predisposition toward learning theory was revealed in their emphasis on the third category; they concluded that ". . . the dominant prong in the process seems to be assimilation, for in all these experiments it is evident that past experience, linguistic habit, cultural forms of thought, and personal motives and attitudes set the stage for the pattern of distortion that occurs and determine just what shall be leveled out and what sharpened" (p. 144).

However, it seems to me that such phenomena can be better conceptualized as active constructions *based upon* a schema organization rather than as the reproduction *of* a trace system even with widespread assimilation. The emphasis is thus placed more on the articulating, abstracting, and comprehending aspect of the process.

What sort of concept is schema? Where does it fall in psychological theory?

Zangwill (1937) has shown that the concept of schema overlaps with the concept of "set." This fact, however, does not make the concept very precise, since, in spite of the fact that set is a ubiquitous concept in psychology, Gibson (1941), after thorough study, found that any common core of meaning was surprisingly difficult to isolate. The concept of set arose in the Würzburg school of psychology because, in their studies of such simple phenomena as reaction time, it was clear that S's reaction was frequently determined by his aim rather than by the stimuli or their associative tendencies. The idea of set, propounded to account for this finding, was conceived of as distinct from association, from reaction, and from ordinary "conscious contact." However, as Gibson points out, the concept has subsequently been defined and used in many ways, and ". . . the assumption that attitudes are determinants which are *external* to learning and also to action has persisted for forty years side-by-side with the contradictory assumption that attitudes are products of learning and are forms of action" (1941, p. 783).

It becomes clear in Gibson's study that the concept, however it is defined and used, refers to the process of thinking. Hebb (1949) has pointed out that the element common to all of the uses of set ". . . is the recognition that responses are determined by something else besides the immediately preceding sensory stimulation" (p. 5). Bartlett made just this point in developing the concept of schema. Hebb calls his "something else" the *autonomous central process* and says it is similar to Morgan's (1943) *central motive state*, Beach's (1942) *central excitatory mechanism*, and Kleitman's (1939) *interest*. Each of these concepts refers to a relatively autonomous component of behavior: a process that must somehow be conceived of as internal to the organism, as having a degree of autonomy from external stimulation, and as playing a more or less central determining role in behavior.

The virtue of Bartlett's schema concept lies in its emphasis that such internal dispositions (which are steadily implicated in behavior) function in neither a passive nor a piecemeal way. Rather their influence takes the form of such active processes as seeking "meaning" (i.e., connectedness), striving after "fit" (i.e., context), and the like. The term set, since it connotes a preparatory activity, seems at once less active and too general and all-embracing, referring as it often does to postures of a purely muscular and physical kind. The term schema, on the other hand, is more dynamic while also more limited, and designates only cognitive factors that not only prepare but, by means of fractionation and recruitment, also shape and assimilate experience.

I have borrowed the terms fractionation and recruitment from Hebb (1949) and, as I have used these concepts, they correspond roughly to the Gestalt processes of sharpening, leveling, and assimilation respectively. In spite of the fact that they are still vague and ill-defined conceptions, I found them useful for understanding the reorganization and rearticulation of schemas as revealed in the reproductions—a way of conceptualizing the many importations, substitutions, fragmentations, and skeletonizations which clustered around the gaps, ambiguities, and less familiar parts of the story. The relationship that emerged between explication and importation is instructive in this regard, because both had the general effect of enhancing redundancy and both frequently seemed to converge on the recruitment process.

Some importations seemed to serve no other function than to *sharpen*; i.e., those which merely emphasized, added color, or the like, without explaining, clarifying, or relating the material. Nevertheless, the majority of importations seemed clearly to have an explicatory function. I would stress the finding that only those importations which were explicatory seemed materially to influence subsequent reproductions and play a conspicuous facilitating role. The role of importations, the conditions under which they will take one form or the other, and the way they coordinate with fractionation to serve the economy of schema formation and operation, need further study.

Individual Differences in Retention and Reproduction

I systematically studied two individual difference variables—retention ability and importation tendency—both of which proved to be relatively stable and relatively independent properties of Ss. At the beginning of this monograph, I contended that Bartlett's failure to concern himself with the "detailed workings" of schemas was related to his lack of concern with veridicality and with fundamental individual differences. To what extent, then, has my concern with these variables revealed such "detailed workings"?

The main result of my search for individual differences was the attention I came to pay to processes which revealed fractionation and recruitment, and to the over-all structural coherence of stimuli. An S's ability to form, use, and maintain the structure of schemas seemed only partly an outcome of his access to appropriate schemas in the form of knowledge about the stimulus experience; it also depended on his mode of schema functioning. On these questions, however, my findings are no more than suggestive and further experiments are needed to learn whether individuals may vary independently with respect to content and style, and how the two are interrelated.

Retention ability is, without doubt, a highly complex variable. Many parameters will need to be studied before we have a fuller understanding of it. Research may need to take into account the possibility that, in addition to different memory modalities (Wallach and Auerbach, 1955), there are various kinds of memory, e.g., digit span—the individual's ability to retain experience for a brief time span to which James applied the concept of short-term memory which ". . . comes to us as belonging to the rearward portion of the present space of time, and not to the genuine past" (1890, p. 647). The genuine past is the province of long-term memory where the effects of experience are learned and retained,

There has also been some recent speculation that a fifteen-minute variety of memory also exists as an independent ability.

A number of experimental and theoretical questions arise: (1) Does the same ability underlie these types of memory? (2) How are they related to each other, e.g., what learning principles are involved in the development of long-term memory from short-term memory? With regard to the first question, the present studies pointed up a positive correlation between retention ability and I.Q., suggesting that there is a broad ability parameter which underlies retention ability. One may speculate that such variables as ability to image and fantasy, available vocabulary, willingness to cooperate in an intellectual task, and the like, are also related to retention ability.

With regard to importation, my findings were unequivocal in their testimony to its validity as a parameter of individual difference. However, with regard to two subsidiary questions, they were inconclusive though highly suggestive: (1) concerning the function of importing in importers and in nonimporters; and (2) concerning the relationship between importation style and the presence of explication in a stimulus.

As I have repeatedly indicated, importing sometimes was clearly explicatory in function (assimilating and connecting), at other times merely decorative and extraneous (sharpening). Interestingly enough, for the nonimporters it rarely seemed to be the latter; most of the decorative importations were contributed by the importers. Moreover, though for the most part the importations that occurred on the unfamiliar and unexplicated stimulus stories were explicatory in nature, the importers' importations on the original version in Experiment III were largely decorative.

Experiments II and III produced conflicting results concerning the relationship between importation and explication: in one case explication benefited the nonimporters more than the importers, while in the other case the reverse was true. The former finding suggested that importation and explication are congruent and overlapping—the importers benefited not as much because their own importations were explicatory. The latter finding suggested that a differential assimilation may have occurred as a result of the "fit" between the importers' schema organization and the organization

CONCLUSIONS AND IMPLICATIONS 145

of the stimulus. To resolve this contradiction, further research is needed to determine when explication will favor importers, and when it will favor nonimporters.

I have conceived of cognitive style as the temporal-sequential and structural patterning of schemas—broadly, as their ongoing processes of operation. It follows therefore that styles are not all-or-none affairs, present in some and absent in others; rather they represent varying degrees of reliance upon what are basic cognitive processes. Styles are used by all individuals under certain extreme stimulus conditions, while in other situations individual differences will emerge. Most *S*s did some importing when the stimulus story was gappy, ambiguous, and too long to be memorized. Most of them also showed skeletonization. However, only with respect to importing was I able to devise a test that can maximize the process, provide quantifiable indices of it, and so permit individual differences to be assessed reliably. A technique needs to be worked out which can do the same for skeletonization.

What other cognitive styles may be involved in remembering? I explored the use and retention of imagery, and this too may deserve further study. In addition, the reproductions also gave indications of another possible style: certain *S*s seemed to strive after the meaning or structure of the stimulus, while others strove primarily for detail.[29] It might be profitable to study good retainers who grasp and capture the character and essence of the stimulus material, and compare them with good retainers who do not. Perhaps a style is reflected here that is partly independent of importation-skeletonization, one that might be termed a global versus

---

[29] Gomulicki (1956) recently conducted a systematic study of qualitative individual differences in the recall of meaningful material. He succeeded in isolating two recall types: he calls them *changers* and *condensers*. The one tends to alter material in recall, the other tends to omit material. The former probably overlaps significantly with my importation category. In this respect note Gomulicki's finding that ". . . one effect of the changers' efforts not to omit anything of consequence was that they introduced extraneous material, or repeated themselves half again as often as did the condensers . . ." (1956, p. 395).

Gomulicki, incidentally, presents a review of the various dichotomies and categories psychologists have suggested to differentiate people with regard to their manner of recall. Among them are Binet's "describers" versus "observers," Stern's "preservers" versus "reorganizers" (Stern observed that certain individuals are inclined to give a simple enumeration of disconnected features of their experiences, while others spin a yarn in which explanation and evaluation are all mixed up in the report itself), and Katona's persons who rely on "individual traces" of discrete items versus those who rely on "structural traces" of organized idea systems.

specific style. There was also a suggestion in the reproductions of some individual differences in how Ss dealt with the emotional components of the stimulus; some syncopated and distorted it, others leveled and erased it.

This leads to the final problem: the relationship between schemas, cognitive styles, and personality as a whole. It seems likely that certain personality types will be found to accompany certain styles.[30] When a psychologist turns his attention to problems of personality theory today, he is likely to think in psychoanalytic terms. Psychoanalytic practice and theory—a theory that has unquestionably exerted a profound influence upon psychology as a whole—offers the most comprehensive as well as the most challenging body of ideas in this field. It might therefore be a step in the direction of theoretical richness and completeness if we could integrate the concept of schema with some of the central psychoanalytic concepts and show how cognitive style may fit into its framework. It will be my aim to show that schemas may profitably be conceived of as *ego apparatuses*, or as structures in the realm of conflict-free ego functioning, in Hartmann's sense of the term (see Rapaport, 1951). To do this necessitates a discussion of some recent ideas in psychoanalytic theory.

Although psychoanalysis gives a central position to memory, nowhere in its vast literature is there an attempt to advance a systematic theory of remembering.[31] There is good reason to suppose that such a theory had to wait for the development of psychoanalytic ego psychology. Before ego psychology, the emphasis of psychoanalysis was more on forgetting than on remembering—its concepts were best suited for this task; e.g., the concepts of censorship and defense, of unconscious impulse and conflict.

Hartmann (1939) was the first to recognize that a comprehensive theory of remembering must take into account the conflict-free sphere of the ego which functions with structured and

---

[30] Stern (1938), for example, claims that there are countless people in whose consciousness the past has little temporal organization, and so mixture and blurrings occur. It can be conjectured that these people are hysterics who rely heavily upon recruitment.

[31] Lewy and Rapaport (1944) come closest to undertaking this task in a paper that set out to clarify the psychoanalytic conception of memory and show its relationship to "academic" memory theories. See also Rapaport's more recent contributions (1951, 1957, 1958).

stable apparatuses. On the whole, one can associate psychoanalytic ego psychology with a growing emphasis on the role of relatively stable and autonomous intrapsychic structures. For example, Klein's intention (1951, 1954) is to show how the effect of drives and needs upon perception is channeled by structures—what he calls styles or system-principles—even though many of these structures are themselves probably crystallizations of recurring motivational states.

This process of crystallization or structure formation is a central and crucial learning phenomenon. Hartmann has described it in these words: "An attitude which arose originally in the service of defense against an instinctual drive may, in the course of time, become an independent structure, in which case the instinctual drive merely triggers this automatized apparatus . . . but, as long as the automatization is not controverted, [the drive] does not determine the details of its action. Such an apparatus may . . . through a change of function turn from being a means into a goal in its own right" (1939, p. 26).

Hartmann has proposed the concept of *automatization* to denote the process by which ego apparatuses in general and cognitive structures in particular are formed. The term is most directly applicable to motor activities, where, with increasing exercise of an action, the intermediate links disappear from consciousness. Hartmann assumes, however, that automatization applies not only to the motor apparatus, but also to perception and thinking as well.

The term automatization seems to have unfortunate connotations. For example, it suggests the mechanical and static properties of learned behavior. Nevertheless Hartmann's formulation may be applicable to the process of schema formation, and may serve to give us a sense of how these internal structures are genetically and topographically related to motivations and to drive dynamics in general.

By conceiving of schemas as ego apparatuses, we provide ourselves with a conceptual tool that can deal with changes in cognitions along the entire scale of transformations: from flagrant distortions of an autistic kind at one end to reality-oriented (i.e., "good") changes of a rationalizing and explicating kind at the other. At the former end of the scale is a loss of autonomy with a corresponding invasion (recruitment) into schema structure of drive and drive-related schemas—perhaps a regression to an earlier developmental stage. At the other end are schemas functioning with a minimum of intrusion from drive and drive-related schemas, but with a recruitment of conceptually related schemas. The distinction is between drive-related and conceptually related schemas.

Klein's structural concept, "style," also has overtones which the alternate term "system-principle" does not. Nevertheless I have used it in this monograph because it is less unwieldy and because some of the extra connotations seem desirable at this point. The concept provides a way to conceptualize an important dimension of schema operation, namely, the temporally extended mode of operation of schemas. Moreover it may provide a way to understand the roots and functions of this parameter.[32]

In addition to these concepts and ideas, there are two general and basic ideas in psychoanalysis which might profitably be applied to learning theory in general and to memory in particular. One is the basic distinction between structure and cathexis, the other is the assumption of a hierarchical layering of all psychic functioning. With regard to the latter, Rapaport has stressed two fundamental kinds of organization: a drive organization and a conceptual organization. He writes: "Memories are originally (early in the life of an organism) organized around drives and arise in consciousness as representations of these drives when drive-tension rises. Later on, as the pertinence of the memory to partial drives is established, this drive-organization yields to the conceptual organization" (1951, p. 630).

These two organizations are related to Freud's concepts of *primary* and *secondary process* (1900). The drive organization of memory operates by the primary process, where the laws of logic do not apply, and ". . . ideas belong with a drive and all of its representations." Then the secondary process comes into play and

[32] Dr. R. R. Holt has raised the issue of whether style is properly a term for a "specific type of defense" or refers to "conflict-free modes or qualities of adaptation." In a personal communication he writes: "This distinction cannot always be made, and no doubt styles sometimes have the effect of keeping something conflict-free. But one can look at the outcome and ask if there is still evidence of not-wholly-integrated conflict in it—can you distinguish between structurally motivated importations and projective ones? Anyone with some projective inclination and pressing-enough material to project might be expected to do a little, but, as a conflict-free style, importation would be more clearly demonstrated if you could rule out the projective function (via a study of content)." This point has also been made by Klein (1954).

leads to a transition from a drive organization of cognition to a conceptual organization. Rapaport writes: "This transition is parallel to, and an aspect of, the emergence from drive-sources of attitudes, interests, and strivings as one of the implications of reality-testing and the reality principle. Attitudes, interests, etc., are cathectic processes derived from drive cathexes; their regulation . . . [is determined by] the reality principle and . . . defensive ego formations which arise when drive demands meet reality demands" (Rapaport, 1951, p. 630).

An important idea that permeates psychoanalytic thinking is that the various psychological forces and modes of organization do not replace one another, but rather in some fashion exist side by side. For example, Rapaport writes that, while the conceptual organization itself becomes progressively more autonomous and comes to consist of a hierarchic layering of organization in which the laws of drive organization are balanced against each other, and while this balance progressively shifts with the rising level of hierarchy toward preponderance of the laws of realistic logical organization, nevertheless an ideal purity of these is never achieved. According to Rapaport, the balance achieved between the two memory organizations is an internalized expression of the balance between the needs of the organism and the potentialities of the environment. It is also the balance between neutralized cathexes (i.e., energy distributions which have become autonomous from their drive source) and cathexes of partial or no neutralization.

While all of these ideas and formulations provide a framework for a learning theory, it must be reiterated that no explicit principles of learning or of structure formation exist in psychoanalytic theory. Hartmann shows how automatization may be fitted into the psychoanalytic framework and has a good deal to say about the conditions under which automatisms are suspended or fixated. But as for the principles which govern the formation and specific operation of automatisms and how automatisms function in their relatively conflict-free condition, he does not specify. Klein's styles can be demonstrated in perceptual research, and prove to be crucial to understanding the influence of needs and motives upon perception. However, just like Bartlett's schemas, their particular mode of operation is still unspecified, and is a promising and important subject for research.

BIBLIOGRAPHY

Allport, G. W. & Postman, L. (1947), *The Psychology of Rumor*. New York: Holt.
Babcock, H. (1930), An Experiment in the Measurement of Mental Deterioration. *Arch. Psychol., N.Y.*, No. 117, pp. 105.
Bartlett, F. C. (1932), *Remembering*. Cambridge: Cambridge University Press.
Beach, F. A. (1942), Analysis of Factors Involved in the Arousal, Maintenance and Manifestation of Sexual Excitement in Male Animals. *Psychosom. Med.*, 4:173-198.
Belbin, E. (1950), The Influence of Interpolated Recall upon Recognition. *Quart. J. Exp. Psychol.*, 2:163-167.
Brain, W. R. (1950), The Concept of the Schema in Neurology and Psychiatry. In D. Richter (Ed.), *Perspectives in Neuropsychiatry*. London: Lewis.
Clark, K. B. (1940), Some Factors Influencing the Remembering of Prose Material. *Arch. Psychol., N.Y.*, No. 253, pp. 1-73.
Davis, D. R. & Sinha, D. (1950), The Effect of One Experience upon the Recall of Another. *Quart. J. Exp. Psychol.*, 2: 43-52.
Deese, J. & Hardman, G. W. (1954), An Analysis of Errors in Retroactive Inhibition of Rote Verbal Learning. *Amer. J. Psychol.*, 67: 299-307.
Estes, W. K. (1956), Learning. *Ann. Rev. Psychol.*, 7: 1-38.
Freud, S. (1900), *The Interpretation of Dreams*. New York: Basic Books, 1955.
Gibson, J. J. (1941), A Critical Review of the Concept of Set in Contemporary Experimental Psychology. *Psychol. Bull.*, 38:781-813.
Gomulicki, B. R. (1953), The Development and Present Status of the Trace Theory of Memory. *Brit. J. Psychol., Mongr. Suppl.*, 29:1-94.
────── (1956), Individual Differences in Recall. *J. Pers.*, 24:387-400.
Granit, A. R. (1921), A Study on the Perception of Form. *Brit. J. Psychol.*, 12:223-247.
Hanawalt, N. G. (1937), Memory Trace for Figures in Recall and Recognition. *Arch. Psychol., N.Y.*, No. 216, pp. 89.
Harris, Z. S. (1952), Discourse Analysis. *Language*, 28:1-30.
────── (1954), Distributional Structure. *Word*, 10:146-162.
Harrower, M. R. (1933), Organization in Higher Mental Processes. In *Smith College Studies in Psychology*, No. 4. Northampton, Mass., pp. 381-444.
Hartmann, H. (1939), *Ego Psychology and the Problem of Adaptation*. New York: International Universities Press, 1958.
Head, H. (1920), *Studies in Neurology*, 2 Vols. London: Hodder & Stoughton and Oxford University Press.
Hebb, D. O. (1949), *The Organization of Behavior*. New York: Wiley.
────── & Foord, E. N. (1945), Errors of Visual Recognition and the Nature of the Trace. *J. Exp. Psychol.*, 35:335-348.
Hilgard, E. R. (1948), *Theories of Learning*. New York: Appleton-Century-Crofts.
James, W. (1890), *The Principles of Psychology*. New York: Holt, 1950.
Katona, G. (1940), *Organizing and Memorizing*. New York: Columbia University Press.
Kirkpatrick, C. (1932), A Tentative Study in Experimental Social Psychology. *Amer. J. Sociol.*, 38:194-206.

Klein, G. S. (1951), The Personal World Through Perception. In *Perception: An Approach to Personality,* eds. R. R. Blake & G. V. Ramsey. New York: Ronald Press, pp. 328-355.
———— (1954), Need and Regulation. In *Nebraska Symposium on Motivation,* ed. M. R. Jones. Lincoln, Nebr.: University of Nebraska Press, pp. 224-274.
Kleitman, N. (1939), *Sleep and Wakefulness.* Chicago: University of Chicago Press.
Koffka, K. (1935), *Principles of Gestalt Psychology.* New York: Harcourt.
Köhler, W. (1929), *Gestalt Psychology.* New York: Liveright.
Lashley, K. S. (1930), Basic Neural Mechanisms in Behavior. *Psychol. Rev.,* 37:1-24.
———— (1952), Comments on W. Penfield's: Memory Mechanisms. *Arch. Neurol. Psychiat.,* 67:178-198.
Levitt, E. E. (1956), A Methodological Study of the Preparation of Connected Verbal Stimuli for Quantitative Memory Experiments. *J. Exp. Psychol.,* 52:33-38.
Lewy, E. & Rapaport, D. (1944), The Psychoanalytic Concept of Memory and Its Relation to Recent Memory Theories. *Psychoanal. Quart.,* 13:16-42.
McGeoch, J. A. & Irion, A. L. (1952), *The Psychology of Human Learning.* New York: Longmans, Green.
———— & McDonald, W. T. (1931), Meaningful Relation and Retroactive Inhibition. *Amer. J. Psychol.,* 43:579-588.
———— & McGeoch, G. O. (1936), Studies in Retroactive Inhibition: VI. The Influence of Relative Serial Positions of Interpolated Synonyms. *J. Exp. Psychol.,* 19:1-23.
———— & McKinney, F. (1934), Retroactive Inhibition in the Learning of Poetry. *Amer. J. Psychol.,* 46:19-33.
McNemar, Q. (1949), *Psychological Statistics.* New York: Wiley & Sons.
Miller, G. A. & Selfridge, J. A. (1950), Verbal Context and the Recall of Meaningful Material. *Amer. J. Psychol.,* 63:176-186.
Morgan, C. T. (1943), *Physiological Psychology.* New York: McGraw-Hill.
Newman, E. G. (1939), Forgetting of Meaningful Material During Sleep and Waking. *Amer. J. Psychol.,* 52:65-71.
Noble, C. E. (1955), The Effect of Familiarization upon Serial Verbal Learning. *J. Exp. Psychol.,* 49:333-338.
Northway, M. L. (1940), The Concept of the "Schema." Parts I & II. *Brit. J. Psychol.,* 30:316-325; 31:22-36.
Oldfield, R. C. (1954), Memory Mechanisms and the Theory of Schemata. *Brit. J. Psychol.,* 45:14-23.
———— & Zangwill, O. L. (1942/43), Head's Concept of the Schema and Its Application in Contemporary British Psychology. Part I: Head's Concept of the Schema. Part II: Critical Analysis of Head's Theory. Part III: Bartlett's Theory of Memory. Part IV: Wolter's Theory of Thinking. *Brit. J. Psychol.,* 32:267-286; 33:58-64; 33:113-129; 33:143-149.
Postman, L. & Rau, L. (1957), Retention as a Function of the Method of Measurement. *Univ. Calif. Publ. in Psych.,* 8:217-270.
Rapaport, D. (1942), *Emotions and Memory,* 2nd ed. New York: International Universities Press, 1950.
———— (Ed.) (1951), *Organization and Pathology of Thought.* New York: Columbia University Press.
———— (1957), Cognitive Structures. In *Contemporary Approaches to Cognition.* Cambridge: Harvard University Press.
———— (1958), The Theory of Ego Autonomy: A Generalization. *Bull. Menninger Clin.,* 22:13-35.

Stern, W. (1938), *General Psychology from the Personalistic Standpoint*. New York: Macmillan.
Tresselt, M. E. & Spragg, S. D. S. (1941), Changes Occurring in the Serial Reproduction of Verbally Perceived Materials. *J. Genet. Psychol.*, 58:255-264.
Wallach, H. & Auerbach, E. (1955), On Memory Modalities. *Amer. J. Psychol.*, 68:249-257.
Werner, H. & Kaplan, B. (1956), The Developmental Approach to Cognition: Its Relevance to the Psychological Interpretation of Anthropological and Ethnolinguistic Data. *Amer. Anthrop.*, 58:866-880.
Williams, M. (1950), The Effects of Experimentally Induced Needs upon Retention. *J. Exp. Psychol.*, 40:139-151.
Winch, W. H. (1911), Some Relations between Substance Memory and Productive Imagination in School Children. *Brit. J. Psychol.*, 4:95-125.
Wolters, A. W. (1933), On Conceptual Thinking. *Brit. J. Psychol.*, 24:133-143.
Woodrow, H. (1940), Interrelations of Measures of Learning. *J. Psychol.*, 10:49-73.
——— (1946), The Ability to Learn. *Psychol. Rev.*, 53:147-158.
Woodworth, R. S. (1938), *Experimental Psychology*. New York: Holt.
Wulf, F. (1922), Über die Veränderung von Vorstellungen (Gedächtnis und Gestalt). *Psychol. Forsch.*, 1:333-373.
Zangwill, O. L. (1937), A Study of the Significance of Attitude in Recognition. *Brit. J. Psychol.*, 28:12-17.

ABOUT THE AUTHOR

I. H. PAUL received his M.A. from McGill University (1950) and his Ph.D. in psychology from the University of Pennsylvania (1954). He was a Fellow at the Austen Riggs Center, Stockbridge, Massachusetts, from 1953 to 1956. Since that time he has been on the faculty of the Psychology Department at New York University and on the staff of its Research Center for Mental Health.

ERRATUM

The >'s should be <'s in Tables 8 (p. 86), 10 (p. 93), 11 (p. 95), 12 (p. 97), 15 (p. 110), 16 (p. 112), and 18 (p. 115).